1492 AN ONGOING VOYAGE

Atlantic World Map. In Battista Agnese [*Portolan Atlas*] Venice, ca. 1544. Vellum Chart Collection, Geography and Map Division. (See also pages 54 and 83.)

Battista Agnese's rendering of the Atlantic world, bounded by Europe and Africa on the east and America on the west, reflected a growing interdependence.

1492

AN ONGOING VOYAGE

JOHN R. HEBERT EDITOR

LIBRARY OF CONGRESS WASHINGTON 1992

⊗The paper used in this publication meets the requirements
for permanence established by
the American National Standard for Information Sciences
"Permanence of Paper for Printed Materials" (ANSI Z39.48–1984).

Library of Congress Cataloging-in-Publication Data
1492 : an ongoing voyage.
p.   cm.
Catalog of a quincentenary exhibition held Aug.-Dec. 1992 at the
Library of Congress.
Includes bibliographical references and index.
ISBN 0–8444–0696–1
Copy 3 Z663 .A713 1992
1. Columbus, Christopher—Exhibitions. 2. America—Discovery and
exploration—Spanish—Exhibitions. 3. Indians—First contact with
Western civilization—Exhibitions. I. Library of Congress.
II. Title: Fourteen ninety-two. III. Title: One thousand four
hundred ninety-two.
E111.A12 1992
970.01'5—dc20   91–34419
                                                          CIP

The symbol used in the chapter openings is a modified version of a glyph, possibly a
place glyph, which appears on the Oztoticpac [Mexico] Land Map of 1540. *Geography
and Map Division.*

Cover: Tribute, including a banner with Madonna and Child. *Huejotzingo Codex.* 1531.

Designed by Stephen Kraft

For sale by the U.S. Government Printing Office
Superintendent of Documents, Mail Stop: SSOP, Washington, DC 20402-9328

CONTENTS

LIST OF ILLUSTRATIONS

FOREWORD

WITH THE 500TH ANNIVERSARY of Columbus's voyage of 1492, we have an opportunity to reflect on the significance of an event that, however it may now be interpreted, was a milestone in the history of humankind. This show, 1492: An Ongoing Voyage, is an attempt to describe that dramatic event, its context, and its effects.

The exhibition is not just about a man called Columbus but about the extraordinary epoch in which he played a role. It explores the worlds of America and the Mediterranean at a time when both were immersed in political and cultural changes. Mining the riches of the Library of Congress, with significant items from foreign collections, the exhibition's curators take us to the so-called Atlantic world, from roughly 1450 to 1600. By design, they extend their coverage after Columbus's voyage by a century to encompass the evolution of the Americas after that first encounter on the shores of San Salvador in the autumn of 1492.

Ever since it acquired the historical collections of Thomas Jefferson, the Library of Congress has gathered materials in many formats that greatly illuminate the societies of the fifteenth and sixteenth centuries. With original codices from Middle America and many contemporary accounts of the Americas and the Mediterranean, as well as a fine collection of the ever-changing maps that helped shape popular views, the Library of Congress is well equipped to address the historical themes associated with the Quincentenary of Columbus's voyage.

We are deeply grateful to the Congress of the United States for its staunch support of the Columbus Quincentenary Program. The exhibition and this catalog stand as tangible proof of the Congress's continuing interest in reviewing our history in order to understand more fully our present circumstances and to prepare for the future.

Our guest curators of 1492: An Ongoing Voyage, Prof. Ida Altman (University of New Orleans) and Prof. John Fleming (Princeton University), have canvassed every section of the Library of Congress to uncover important documents related to the period. These treasures, appearing in many different formats and languages, are represented throughout the catalog and the exhibition.

Our Quincentenary effort has drawn heavily upon the Library of Congress's greatest assets: its librarians, archivists, conservators, curators, managers, writers, editors, and photographers. Their talents have been enlisted by the staff of the Library's Quincentenary program, led by its coordinator,

John R. Hébert. The result is a program of exhibitions, publications, film series, scholarly programs, and educational outreach efforts scheduled through 1993.

Through major programs, such as this one, we are striving to make the riches of this great national institution more available to more Americans than ever before.

James H. Billington
The Librarian of Congress

EXHIBITION PARTICIPANTS

Curator
JOHN R. HEBERT

Exhibit Director
BARBARA M. LOSTE

Guest Curators
IDA ALTMAN
JOHN FLEMING

Research Specialists
LEE K. MILLER
ANTHONY PAEZ MULLAN

Office Manager
ROBERT L. ROY

Designer
CHRIS WHITE DESIGN, INC.

Writer
SARA DAY

Photo Research
ANN MONROE JACOBS
CORINNE SZABO

Development
PAT GRAY
MOLLY LEUCHTNER

Interpretive Programs Officer
IRENE U. BURNHAM

Registrars
TAMBRA JOHNSON
KATHLEEN TOBIN

ACKNOWLEDGMENTS

THE RECOGNITION OF THE 500TH anniversary of Christopher Columbus's historic meeting with the people on the island of Guanahani, in the Bahamas, on October 12, 1492, provides us the opportunity to examine carefully the events leading up to and following that complicated encounter. The Library of Congress's Quincentenary Program, An Ongoing Voyage, is a major interpretive effort which features exhibitions, publications, film series, scholarly programs, and educational outreach projects. Through these varied undertakings, we are allowed to consider, in broad terms, the impact of that unexpected cultural interaction that occurred 500 years ago and the continuing consequences of that contact in our very lives.

The beginning of the An Ongoing Voyage program can be traced to the growing sentiment during the 1980s within the Library of Congress and in the scholarly community for a form of recognition, a commemoration of the 500th anniversary of Columbus's voyage to America that would include scholarly exchanges on various facets of that historical period. With a special appropriation from Congress, begun in fiscal year 1989, An Ongoing Voyage, the Quincentenary Program of the Library of Congress, was formed. The program has received encouragement and unwavering support from a vast number of individuals and institutions, all of whom have made the Library's Quincentenary Program possible.

An Ongoing Voyage is dedicated to the creative use of the Library's collections and specialists. Highlights of the program include the major 1992 exhibition, 1492: An Ongoing Voyage; *The Hispanic World 1492–1898,* a survey of microfilm and other photoreproduced holdings in U.S. institutions of archival documents from Spain; Library of Congress Quincentenary research guides, including one on Columbus and the Age of Exploration (*Keys to the Encounter*) and another on the American Indian materials in the Library of Congress; the Italians in the U.S. West documentary project; facsimiles of treasures in the Library of Congress's collections; the 1990 and the 1992 Educator's Institutes for secondary school social science teachers; an hour-length film of Columbus, *Christopher Columbus: The Ongoing Voyage,* prepared by the Library's Global Library Project; and conferences, including An Ongoing Voyage: Music, in collaboration with the Library's Music Division.

None of these undertakings could have been planned and completed without the support of numerous individuals and institutions, starting with Librarian of Congress James H. Billington. John Cole, Acting Associate Librarian for Cultural Affairs and his staff, especially Sharon Green, John Kozar, Roberta Stevens, and Jackie Wintle, have provided continuing encouragement. Declan Murphy, Special Assistant to the Librarian, provided helpful early support to the Library's efforts.

The very valuable assistance and cooperation of the Library's Interpretive Programs Office, and its director Irene Burnham, from securing loan items for the exhibit to critical matters regarding design, fabrication, and installation, must be recognized; we are especially appreciative of the professional assistance of Andy Cosentino, Debbie Durbeck, Tambra Johnson, Kimberly Lord, Gene Roberts, Edward Rosenfeld, and Kathleen Tobin. Our project began when Diantha Schull directed the Interpretive Programs Office, and her encouragement led to many of our future program initiatives.

A number of individuals and institutions have helped us in the preparation of the exhibition and other elements of our program. A listing of every person and every institution who affected our program and this exhibition would fill pages and still be incomplete. This fact in no way lessens our deep appreciation for the spirit of cooperation and rich scholarly exchange that has been evidenced throughout the development of the program. The collection specialists in the Library of Congress have been active supporters of our inquiry regarding collections and Quincentenary materials. Not only for the exhibition and the exhibition catalog, but also for the Educator's Institute, the Spanish archival survey project, and the guides to collections, the reference specialists and the administration of the Geography and Map, Manuscript, Prints and Photographs, Rare Book and Special Collections, Hispanic, General Reading Rooms, European, African and Middle Eastern, Asian, Music, and Motion Pictures, Broadcasting, and Recorded Sound Divisions, the American Folklife Center, the Law Library, and the Conservation Office have shared their years of experience and knowledge regarding documents and collections. They all encouraged use of their rich and unparalleled collections to tell our story. One individual, John Wolter, recently retired chief of the Geography and Map Division, deserves special mention; John has remained a trusting friend and delightful mentor as we ventured through the perils along the Quincentenary path.

The Library's Public Affairs Office, especially Helen Dalrymple and John Sullivan, and Publishing Office, particularly Iris Newsom, Johanna Craig, Dana Pratt, and Peggy Wagner, have generously supported our efforts; the important design contributions of Robert Kinneary and Don Shomette do not go unnoticed. Without the help of these individuals the work of the Quincentenary program of the Library of Congress would have been much more arduous, less wide ranging, and probably less effective.

Outside of LC, various libraries and museums—including the Kuntshistorisches Museum (Vienna), the Museum für Völkerkunde (Vienna), Tulane University (and its extraordinary Latin American collections), the Walters Art Gallery (Baltimore), the Smithsonian Institution, the Pierpoint Morgan Library (New York City), the San Antonio Museum of Art, and the Witte Museum (San Antonio), among many others—have been unselfish in suggesting and lending items for our exhibition. The in-depth photo research of Corinne Szabo and Ann Jacobs during the formative stage of exhibit development has been vital. Various private collectors have allowed their treasures to appear in the exhibit; among these individuals was Gary Eyler. In preparing material for the exhibition, Bob Abel of Synapse Technologies gave essential assistance in the early development stage. Several organizations and their outstanding representatives, e.g., Spain '92, the Cultural Offices of the embassies of Spain, Mexico, and Italy, the Quincentenary Program of the Organization of American States, Phi Beta Kappa, the Smithsonian Institution, the National Endowment for the Humanities, the U.S. Christopher Columbus Quincentenary Jubilee Commission, National History Day, and individuals, e.g., Zaida Alcalde, Louis de Vorsey, Jr., Douglas Foard, Alicia González, Joaquin Gonazález Casanova, Guadalupe Jiménez Codinach, Jim Kiernan, Margrit Krewson, Everette Larson, Rafael Mazarrasa, Tony McIvor, Marion Oettinger, Colin Palmer, José Ramón Remacha, Judy Reynolds, Malcolm Richardson, Lynda Schaeffer, Carlo Trezza, Dave Warren, and John Williams have willingly contributed a vast storehouse of wisdom to our endeavors. We are extremely grateful to these talented colleagues.

Most fortuitously, we were able to enlist Chris White Design to assist us with the exhibit design and to count on the talented services of editor-writer Sara Day in the final preparation of text, labels, and explanations. Several key individuals have worked directly with the program from its inception, including Lee K. Miller, who conducted important research about the cultural history of U.S. and Canadian Indian peoples; Pamela Foster, who worked diligently during the summer of 1991 to ensure quality in our presentation; Pat Gray and Mollie Leuchtner who both sought corporate sponsorship for our program; and Lynda Smith who guided the successful Library of Congress-National History Day Educator's Institute of 1990 and who helped us to expand on the necessary educational dimension of our undertaking.

We were fortunate indeed to have as guest curators Ida Altman and John Fleming. Ida and John shared the burden of constructing an interesting story about the meeting of two separate parts of the world—America and Europe—that occurred in 1492. Both brought to the discussion immense talent, great insight, and the desire for historical accuracy which made the work of preparation of the exhibition and the exhibition catalog viable and educational. While both come from different disciplines, Ida from history and John from literature, each is concerned with the educational dimension of the Quincentenary and provided years of wisdom in order to assist us in our understanding of a very complicated and complex history. Each contributed to the exhibition catalog and, along with ethnohistorian James Lockhart (UCLA) and several specialists from the Library of Congress, produced lively and highly readable texts on the history of the 1492 encounter of America and Europe.

Three individuals have remained key to the success of the Quincentenary Program. Anthony Mullan, General Reading Rooms Division, has been a reliable and able researcher for the project, providing skilled and timely assistance to the guest curators and taking as his responsibility bibliographical citations for the exhibition catalog and thoughtful descriptions of key items in the catalog and the exhibition. Tony has been a necessary addition to our small working force and we are indebted to his division for sharing this very talented individual with us. Our office manager, Robert Roy, who keeps all of us in line and informed, deserves much credit for the successes of the program. Rob can manage many and varied requests better than any two persons I know; he has worked long and hard throughout the life of the program to ensure the timely completion of the archival survey project, the Educator's Institute, the exhibition catalog, the exhibition object lists, the contracts associated with the program, and many other office matters. He brings to our program knowledge of the subject, a pleasing manner, and a sense of dedication to getting the job done well.

Finally, I owe a special debt to Barbara Loste, the assistant coordinator of the program. She has been involved in the decision making on projects, on program direction, and in other matters of the Quincentenary initiative of the Library of Congress since the program's inception in March 1989. Barbara has given invaluable insight to the program based on her experience in exhibition design and preparation and publishing, and her practical knowledge of Latin American cultures. She has brought an especially fresh eye to the program and has provided sound assistance and advice on the numerous projects that we have undertaken. She is the key sounding board for project direction and intent. It is a pleasure to have this serious and energetic colleague deeply involved in the initiatives that have become associated with the Library of Congress's Quincentenary Program, An Ongoing Voyage.

Through these individuals and institutions and many more who unfortunately remain unnamed, we have made various successful and unsuccessful attempts to unravel the history of the complex and complicated cultures that met in 1492, as we glimpse through an imperfect rear view mirror at the exciting and personal history surrounding the Columbian voyages to America.

John R. Hébert
Coordinator
The Quincentenary Program

CHAPTER ONE

ᛟᚾ OVERVIEW

by JOHN R. HEBERT

A N HISTORICAL MEETING of two separate and complex parts of the world occurred on October 12, 1492, when Christopher Columbus unwittingly sailed three ships into the Bahamas and into contact with the Taino peoples on the island of Guanahani. Neither group had been aware of the existence of the other. Furthermore, neither had an inkling of the rich and diverse cultures that the other represented. That meeting, that chance encounter, created unexpected cultural interactions between the inhabitants of America and Europe. It set the stage for a series of misunderstandings and misconceptions about each other that would endure for years.

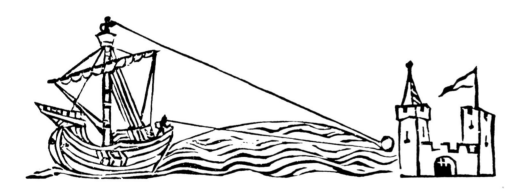

Sighting Land. In Johannes de Sacrobosco. *De Sphaera.* **Venice, 1488. Rosenwald Collection, Rare Book and Special Collections Division.**

Substantial literature had been amassed by the late fifteenth century to make nautical travel understandable to a growing interested public, as exemplified by this standard "how to do it" book.

In 1492: An Ongoing Voyage the Library of Congress has set out to recognize the societies that came into contact and the main actors in that encounter. Columbus's 1493 description of the area that he encountered, which he thought to be part of Asia, excited Europe. Later writings by Vespucci, Martyr, Oviedo, and others cast America in varied lights. Ultimately, interest was widespread to uncover more of this huge landmass. At first, the European explorers were unwilling to acknowledge America's individuality, seeking in many ways to see the area as part of Asia, or later, as an impediment in the path to the riches of China and India. To fifteenth-century Europe, only one sea separated it from Asia, the Atlantic, and it was only long after Columbus died that the existence of two oceans separating the far reaches of Europe's known world was realized.

In spite of this misunderstanding of the American hemisphere, Spaniards, Portuguese, French, English, and Africans arrived to its shores to en-

World Globe with Armillary Sphere. Caspar Vopel, Cologne, 1543. Manuscript. Geography and Map Division.

Terrestrial and celestial globes and armillary spheres were important educational tools for illustrating the geographical, astronomical, and cosmographical concepts of the Renaissance and the Age of European Discovery. Terrestrial globes not only reflected the spherical nature of the earth but, as with other forms of cartography, they served to document man's changing perception and expanding knowledge of the geography of the earth. Globes have an advantage over flat maps in that all places are in their correct position in relation to each other, and the shapes of land and water features adhere to geographic reality. Armillary spheres were demonstration models for teaching astronomy and for illustrating the earth's position within the universe.

This finely crafted and well-preserved three-inch terrestrial globe, within a six-inch armillary sphere, mounted on an octagonal brass base, is the work of Caspar Vopel (1511–1561), a teacher of mathematics in Cologne, Germany, and a scholar of wide cosmographical interests. Germany was the center of the development of globe production in Europe, and Vopel's profession as a mathematician provided skills that could readily be applied to the design and construction of cartographic materials and related instruments. In addition to terrestrial globes and armillary spheres, Vopel's known works include celestial globes, an atlas, maps, and a number of scientific instruments. His production was apparently not large, however, for few copies of his works have survived. For example, no copy remains of his large world map of 1545. Six small globes within armillary spheres, similar to the one illustrated here, are known to exist.

Vopel skillfully drew by hand his portrayal of the earth's surface directly on the globe ball. Of particular historical interest is his portrayal of the uncertainty still prevalent in the first half of the sixteenth century among cosmographers regarding Columbus's contention that he had reached Asia. As shown on the globe, Vopel agreed with the school of thought that North America and Asia were joined as one landmass—a misconception that continued on some maps until the late sixteenth century.

Vopel's armillary sphere presents a model of the Ptolemaic or earth-centered cosmic system. The series of eleven interlocking and overlapping brass rings or armilla, some of which are movable, that make up

counter its complex, varied societies. They took its riches back to the Mediterranean and other parts of Europe or remained to cultivate its soil. They brought with them a variety of cultures from a polyglot Mediterranean and Atlantic Europe.

The joining of the Atlantic world through trade and politics brought America into a long-term relationship with Europe, and a binding interdependence developed. America possessed commodities that Europe sought for its pleasure and its very survival.

New food products from America replenished empty cupboards in Europe. European crops and animals replaced products in America. Tomatoes, potatoes, chocolate, pineapples, peanuts, beans, corn, and tobacco came from America; wheat, cattle, horses, and sugarcane traveled from Europe to America. Various seeds intermingled in alien soil to generate new offsprings.

The arrival of newcomers from Europe in the fifteenth and the sixteenth centuries changed considerably the face of America. In some areas, such as in Mesoamerica and in Peru, Spaniards settled permanently; along the North and South Atlantic coasts of America European settlement and conquest were slowly realized.

And what was the reaction of American societies to the arrival of these newcomers? In 1492, numerous tribes occupied America from the Arctic Circle to Tierra del Fuego. These societies, in most cases, knew little about each other and as little of the whole of America as did the explorers and conquerors from Europe. Their responses to the arrival of Spaniards, Portuguese, French, English, and others varied. While occasionally parallel settlements occurred, in other cases, conflict developed as European peoples attempted to place their cultures on top of existing structures, effectively disrupting long-established living patterns in negative fashion. Enslavement, devastating diseases, warfare, and outright slaughters reduced American populations drastically. In yet other cases, no European contact occurred until

the armillary sphere are adjustable for the seasons and illustrate the circles of the sun, moon, known planets, and important stars. The wide ecliptic band includes delicate engravings of the signs of the zodiac. It is interesting to note that 1543 is not only the year of the construction of Vopel's armillary sphere, but it is also the year Copernicus's theory of a heliocentric universe was published, a theory that greatly changed the design of armillary spheres.

James A. Flatness

West Coast America, ca. 1550. Portolan chart on vellum. Vellum chart collection, 9, Geography and Map Division.

A fragment of a ca. midsixteenth-century chart of the Pacific Coast of America, from Nicaragua to Peru, indicates the growing presence of Spain on the land. Portolan charts were in common use among Mediterranean sailors beginning in the late Middle Ages.

long after the initial voyages of exploration were completed. Life remained relatively unchanged in vast stretches of America. Generally, however, American Indian societies suffered lasting destruction to customs, practices, and spiritual beliefs.

The Columbian voyage, then, was not an end unto itself but the beginning of a 500-year-old experience that has witnessed peoples from all over the globe intermingling in America and acting and reacting in various fashions and with untold consequences towards each other.

In 1992 the world will focus its attention on the 500th anniversary of Columbus's first voyage to the Indies. Thus it is that we have the rare opportunity to reexamine a number of the significant issues that are raised by this historical event. We do not see this opportunity simply as a moment for celebration or as a pretext for gala events. It is, instead, the appropriate occasion to deepen understanding of our rich cultural heritages and our historical and geographical ties with the entire hemisphere.

The Library's 1992 Quincentenary exhibition 1492: An Ongoing Voyage explores the issues surrounding the encounter 500 years ago between America and Europe. It addresses the immediate consequences of Columbus's landing in the Bahamas and suggests that the continuing nature of the encounter can be likened to an ongoing voyage. At the heart of the exhibition is the identification of the unifying links and discordant notes that radically affect accurate perceptions of reality, as individuals and societies sought knowledge and understanding in approaching the unknown.

To these ends, the Library of Congress, relying upon its rich and vast collections, has developed an exhibition, appearing in the Library's Madison Building between August 1992 and January 1993, which includes three major topics. It describes the levels of knowledge existing before contact between America and the Mediterranean world, juxtaposing American Indian peoples' perceptions of themselves in the world with European conceptions and misconceptions of the world on the eve of 1492. It characterizes Christopher Columbus, the Mediterranean navigator, in the context of his world and the progress in nautical and navigational experiences of his time. It portrays the period of the encounter in America, from 1492 to 1600, centering on knowledge, learning, societies, explorers, syncretism, and the differences that persisted between the cultures in contact.

Through the exhibition and this catalog, we have relied upon the vast resources of the Library of Congress, both in its rich collections and in the knowledge of its many specialists, to interpret various Quincentenary themes. In that way, the Library is sending a signal to its public that it contains valuable and essential information which can support study of the rich and unexplored themes linked to the Columbian voyages and the encounter of America and Europe.

The state of knowledge in America and in the Mediterranean world about other peoples, the sophistication of navigational and cartographic tools, the richness and the diversity of cultures in America and in the Mediterranean area in the late fifteenth century, key figures including Christopher Columbus, relationships between Europe and America upon contact in 1492, and the continuing repercussions in American society following the chance meeting of two separate parts of the world in 1492 are subthemes of considerable interest, and these threads bind the exhibit and this catalog.

Library of Congress's Quincentenary Program An Ongoing Voyage logo.

The Library's Quincentenary Program logo represents the encounter and syncretism between different cultures. The cross is similar to that used on the ship sails of the European explorers who at great risk crossed the unknown in search of a westerly route to the Orient. The flames, based on American Indian drawings, represent the sun or the brilliance of America.

Their search for trade routes to Asia brought the Portuguese into contact with West African cultures from the midfifteenth century. Establishing trading posts (factors) on the coast, the Portuguese sought African products, such as ivories, and people, who were enslaved.

The purpose of this catalog is to address the three significant thematic elements mentioned above. Separate chapters of this volume discuss European ideas of other peoples, American Indian societies before 1492, and America after contact. The Columbian voyage linked the world in a fashion unknown to that time. It brought into contact, willingly or unwillingly, peoples who retained prejudices about self worth and others that persist today.

Through various contributions in this catalog we describe America and Europe-Africa as distinctive complex worlds, each formed by diverse historical, literary, and religious traditions.

In the chapter "Life in the Mediterranean World," John Fleming identifies the complex features of the civilization which nourished Columbus, his patrons and collaborators, and those who soon followed in his wake to America. Fleming classifies the Mediterranean world as an ambivalent place, a polyglot diversity and a remarkable unity. He senses that that area was undergoing great stress in confronting the Muslim Turks who were disrupting sea traffic and acquiring territory in Southern Europe. The exception to this phenomenon was in Spain which he views as an optimistic, nationalistically oriented, religiously destined society.

In "Spain in the Era of Exploration," Ida Altman provides a focused survey of the Iberian peninsula in the late fifteenth century. The division of Spain between Christian and Muslim areas in the Middle Ages, she contends, did not always lead to warfare and struggle over opposing religions and cultures. Long periods of relative harmony characterized Iberian life as significant crosscurrents of influence flowed among Christian, Muslim, and Jewish communities. The pluralistic society of the Middle Ages left a legacy of cultural diversity in the Iberian peninsula. By the end of the late Middle Ages, however, momentum shifted in Christian areas to wrest territory from Mus-

Peasant Couple Dancing. Woodcut by Albrecht Dürer, 1471–1528. German. Prints and Photographs Division.

Dürer, a renowned cultural artist and a contemporary of Christopher Columbus, captured the spirit of everyday life in Europe at the turn of the sixteenth century through his numerous graphic representations.

lim control. With Christian reconquest came a strengthening, extension, and centralization of royal power in Spain. Events in 1492 both symbolized and signalled the creation of the orthodox, Christian society that Isabel and Fernando of Spain envisioned.

Any discussion of the Mediterranean world of the time would be incomplete without reference to mapmaking and advances in nautical skill. John Fleming, in "Maps, Navigation, and World Travel," discusses advancements in sea travel. He notes geographic accomplishments in the period, with specific reference to the lasting impact of the cartographic contributions of Clau-

Alcázar, Seville, Spain. Photo.

The lasting impact of Islamic culture in Spain is especially evident in the Andalusian region, the center for Spanish exploration to America. The Alcázar, in the center of Seville, served as the royal residence of the Spanish crown in the early sixteenth century. It is one of many masterpieces of Moorish architecture surviving in Iberia.

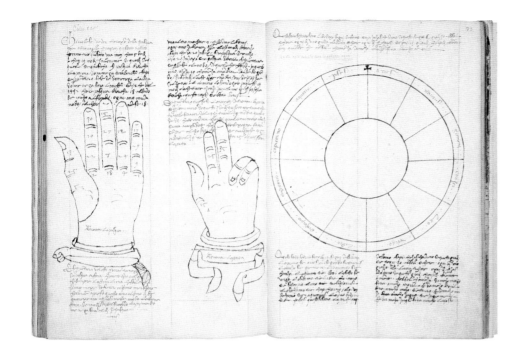

Drawings of zodiacs, hands, and divisions of time in Nicolo Stolfo. [Early Venetian Sailing Directions in the Mediterranean Sea] Manuscript. [Venice] August 1499. Rare Book and Special Collections Division.

By the late fifteenth century an emerging body of literature to facilitate sea travel in the Mediterranean world was available. This early book of sailing directions served as a handy guide for the sailor and a storehouse of practical information for laymen.

dius Ptolemy and the growing body of contemporary practical sea charts, known as portolan charts, that were the indispensable guides for improved travel. This expanding cartographic literature was bolstered in Europe by a fairly extensive library of scientific and pseudoscientific writings on geography, astronomy, cosmology, and navigation. Such writers as Marco Polo and Jean de Mandeville influenced adventurers and explorers during Columbus's time as they provided fanciful notions of "other" world peoples—cannibals, dog-headed men, and one-eyed races—a marvelous grouping of how other people and cultures would appear. Out of this literature emerged sets of perceptions and misconceptions in Europe that affected adversely the understanding of other peoples for decades following 1492.

In "Christopher Columbus, the Man and the Myth," Fleming asserts that it is misleading to commemorate Columbus's voyage of 1492 as a single event since the cultural encounters between Europeans and Americans remained complex, varied, and continual. In response to the frequently posed question of who was Columbus, he suggests that there is no definitive answer, that there are many Columbuses. When an attempt is made to separate the man from the myths, surprising mysteries, contradictions, and uncertainties concerning basic biographical facts are found. Scholars will no doubt continue to search for, and debate will be waged over, the real Columbus.

As a contrast to the chapters on the Mediterranean world, James Lockhart, in "The Indians of the Central Areas When the Europeans Arrived," provides a rich and lucid survey of the societies of Central Mexico and the Andes before the arrival of the Spaniards in the early sixteenth century. He opens with the sobering thought that no word with approximately the same definition as "Indians" or "Native Americans" existed in any indigenous language. No hemisphericwide appreciation of the unity of Indian peoples existed. "The thrust of such terms is to differentiate the inhabitants of the Western Hemisphere from the rest of humanity, and since the peoples we call Indians were unaware of the rest, it follows that they had no need for words

Smoking Tobacco in the New World. In André Thevet. *Les Singularitez de la France Antarctique.* **Paris, 1557. Rare Book and Special Collections Division.**

André Thevet, a French Franciscan priest who served as chaplain with Villegagnon's 1555–56 expedition to Brazil, published three works containing woodcut illustrations of American Indian peoples. His 1557 work, *Les Singularitez de la France Antarctique* included seventeen woodcuts of Brazilian peoples engaged in various activities, e.g., cutting palm and brazilwood trees, harvesting fruit, making the fermented maize beer *chica,* and making fire and smoking a cigar.

relating to them. The Indian peoples of America, North and South, were varied, speaking hundreds of mutually unintelligible languages." Their cultures were as separate and as different from each other as those of ancient Rome and the Picts. Literally hundreds, if not thousands, of discrete Indian societies called America home in 1492.

The most populous groups of the central areas of Mexico and Peru shared the most in common with the Europeans and it is no accident that it was to these groups that the Spanish were attracted. The peoples of Mesoamerica and the Andes were engaged for centuries in intensive agriculture, irrigation, and land reclamation; land ownership was transferred from father to son. People lived in major permanent concentrations, and there were lords and commoners similar to those of Europe.

In "The Contact of Cultures in America," Ida Altman enumerates the forms of contact between Europeans and the Indian societies of the Caribbean, the North Atlantic coast and interior (what is now the United States and Canada), and the South Atlantic coast of Brazil and the Rio de la Plata region. In this geographically broad presentation, she points out that in some cases

Europeans appeared as conquerors of peoples and territories, while in other cases they were wholly dependent on the aid and the tolerance of the local inhabitants. Contact generated a variety of responses on both sides as Tainos, various Indian societies on the North Atlantic coast of America, and the Tupis and Guaranis of the South Atlantic coast encountered Spaniards, English, French, Portuguese, and Africans with differing objectives.

James Lockhart, in "The Central Areas During and After the Conquest," studies the complicated shifting alliances between Indian groups and Spaniards after 1500. He chronicles the manner in which the Iberian conquerors attained control of both Central Mexico and Peru in the early sixteenth century. Ultimately, superior military equipment and lack of alliances among Indian peoples led to their defeat. Following conquest, the Spaniards politically placed themselves atop existing structures. The Spanish and the indigenous peoples' orbits gradually grew into each others' to form a new overall entity, which Lockhart characterizes as the prototype of the nations we see in the region today. In spite of many recognizable changes, the areas of Central Mexico and Peru, the central areas, retained the imprint of the sixteenth century and the flavor of the indigenous world more than most other parts of the Western Hemisphere.

Extending the story beyond the sixteenth century, Barbara Loste points out in the "Epilogue" that changes continue to occur in our racial, cultural, and ethnic makeup as America continues to become the site of a steady stream of immigration and migration from internal and external sources. We are a multicultural society, products of many parts of the world. Out of the Quincentenary observance can emerge a greater appreciation of our broad world heritages that can facilitate existence in our pluralistic society.

Interspersed in the chapters are descriptions of treasures from the Library of Congress's collections which complement the content of the chapters. Library specialists, many of whom are the curators of the collections out of

Cortés and Soldiers Confront the Indians. In Fray Diego Durán. *La Historia antigua de la Nueva España.* 1585. Peter Force Collection, Manuscript Division.

The fierce confrontation between the Spaniards under Cortés and the followers of Montezuma received full treatment in Father Durán's illustrated history of New Spain, compiled shortly after the early sixteenth-century Conquest.

which the specific items came, provided the extended commentary.

The treasures selected for special treatment as sidebars and the additional illustrations sprinkled throughout this volume facilitate understanding of the incredibly complex and diverse parts of the world that America and the

Mediterranean represented in the late fifteenth century. These documents on display in the exhibit and appearing in this catalog are the essential historical records needed for understanding a seemingly far distant past. Without these most valuable records our knowledge of the events of 500 years ago would be woefully incomplete. Through careful use of documents—such as the Huejotzingo Codex (Mexico 1531), the Oztoticpac lands map (Mexico 1540), the sixteenth-century Relación de Michoacan, Christopher Columbus's 1502 manuscript "Book of Privileges," Angelo Trevisan's 1502 manuscript of Spanish and Portuguese voyages of exploration, Ruysch's 1507 world map, Columbus's 1493 letter, Oviedo's first images of American plants and peoples, or Diego Gutiérrez's 1562 monumental map of America—we can relate the story as it happened, and not as we would like it to be.

This catalog acquaints you with the very rich and diverse context that underpins the singular event that prompted the Quincentenary remembrance. The chapters, individually and collectively, provide broader interpretation of the separate parts of the world that became inextricably bound as a result of the 1492 voyage of Columbus and the repeated ventures that followed in its wake. At times the articles are intended to compare and to contrast America with the Mediterranean world; at times it is quite clear that we are speaking about two distinctive, complex parts of the world totally unknown to each other that unwittingly met in 1492. While this catalog cannot duplicate the exhibition entirely, the general themes and many of the documents that appear in the exhibit also appear in it.

During our involvement in the preparations for the 500th anniversary of Columbus's voyages, we have become increasingly sensitive to various interpretations of particular terms. For many of us, words, such as discovery, New World/Old World, America, Indians, and Native Americans, trigger a recognition that we believe others share. How often have we heard that Columbus discovered America? Or that he came to the New World from the Old World? That the people he met were Indians or, now, Native Americans? That we live in America, which when Columbus arrived was a vast wilderness unspoiled by man? Words can and do provoke reactions, reactions to which we are totally unaware.

Discovery, when normally used, has suggested an action which uncovered an unknown place or phenomenon. That understanding with regard to America is far from reality. Those individuals and empires inhabiting America knew they existed, and possibly others did too, so they did not feel "discovered." Through his enterprise Columbus had been seeking a shorter route to a known land, Asia. He, in 1492, unwittingly stumbled upon an area unknown to him and to Europe. His action, in retrospect, was for Europe a discovery of a place unknown to it.

It seems likely that Columbus did not believe in his lifetime that he had reached an unknown part of the world. Only after repeated European contact was made with America did it become discovered, understood to them. In early writings about Spanish exploration of America, reference was made not to discovering the place; the term used in Spanish was *inventar,* which is to make a new thing known to the observer.

One of the modern writers on the contact between America and Europe, Edmundo O'Gorman, follows this logical approach in his 1961 work *The Invention of America.* As O'Gorman points out, the earliest text in which Co-

Prickly Pear Cactus. In Gonzalo Fernández de Oviedo y Valdés. *Corónica de las Indias: La Hystoria general y natural de las Indias.* **Salamanca, 1547. Rare Book and Special Collections Division.**

Iguana. In Gonzalo Fernández de Oviedo y Valdés. *Corónica de las Indias: La Hystoria General y Natural de las Indias.* **Salamanca, 1547. Rare Book and Special Collections Division.**

Chronicler and naturalist Fernández de Oviedo y Valdés spent nearly thirty years in America, including some twenty years in Santo Domingo, beginning in 1514. His many drawings of plants and animals are increased in value by his stated lack of artistic talent which confirms their originality, without embellishment.

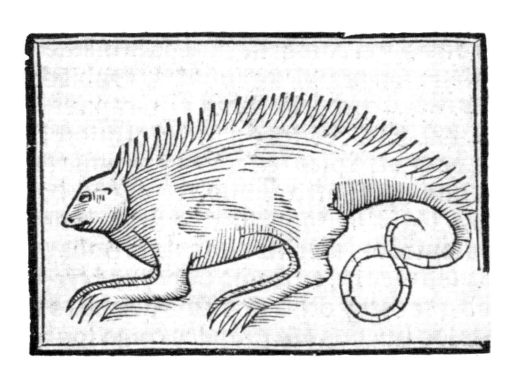

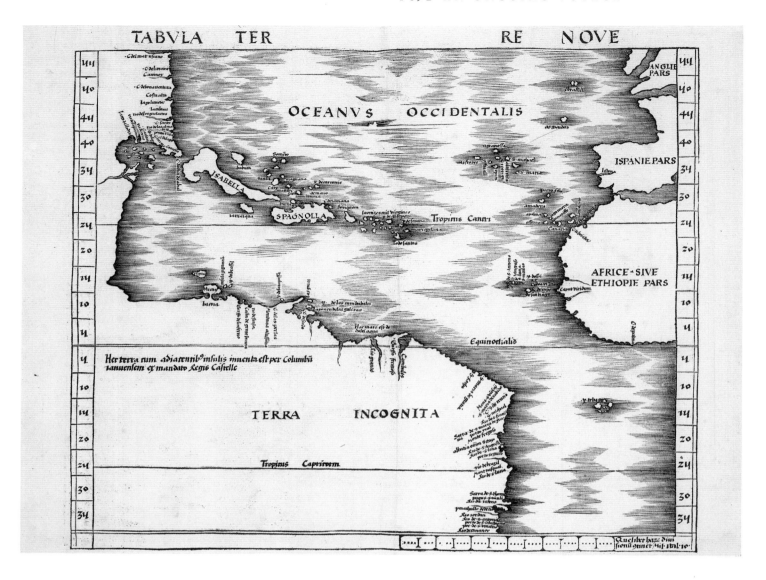

Map of America. Martin Waldseemüller. [Ptolemaeus] *Geographiae Opus Novissima Traductione . . .* **Strasbourg, 1513. Geography and Map Division.**

The first appearance of a map of America in a Ptolemy atlas occurred in the 1513 Strasbourg edition, which included a series of new maps, based on findings from recent European explorations. Martin Waldseemüller of St. Dié began work on this new edition of Ptolemy about 1505 and compiled the maps. In this work, America remains named "Tierra Incognita" and Columbus is credited with informing Fernando and Isabel of its existence.

lumbus appears as the discoverer of America is in Gonzalo Fernández de Oviedo's *Sumario de la historia natural de las Indias* published in 1526, twenty years after Columbus died. And it was nearly the midsixteenth century before European geographers and mapmakers realized that America was a separate continent from the Asia-Europe-Africa landmass.

This leads us to the use of the terms *Old World, New World,* and *America.* In this catalog and in the exhibition we have chosen to refer to the Western Hemisphere as America, not as the New World. While both terms occurred after contact between Europeans and Americans had begun, to use the term *New World* would be to continue to recognize a European-centered perception of old and new. The Western Hemisphere may have been new to Europeans but old, very old, to those who resided here. Full-blown empires were active in America before the birth of Christ.

America, as a term, is no more historically correct than New World, but it is preferred because it is less used as a comparison of age of land and peoples. There was no universal term for the space occupied by the people Columbus met. Therefore, America refers to an entity that is given unity after 1500 and it derives from the reference to Amerigo Vespucci's explora-

[34]

tions and startling assertion that a distinctive continent had been touched by Columbus in 1492. Even then, the full extent of America was not fully appreciated as an independent area, not attached to Asia. In our use of the name America, we refer to the entire area known as the Western Hemisphere, completely separated from the Eastern Hemisphere, Asia-Europe-Africa.

The inhabitants of America, called Indian peoples or Native Americans, had no unifying term for themselves in 1492 and, seemingly, no need for one. Those who lived in fifteenth-century Europe were accustomed to calling themselves Europeans or Christians. The Western Hemisphere, stretching from Tierra del Fuego to the Arctic Circle, was home for diverse civilizations, empires, tribes, millions of peoples who did not have a common knowledge of each other. The name Indians, mistakenly applied to the peoples of the Caribbean by Columbus, became the European name for the inhabitants of the entire hemisphere. Debates continue today over the use or misuse of the terms *Indian,* or *Native American.* We have chosen, instead, to use the names by which individual peoples were known, such as Mexica, Tlaxcalan, Incas, Tainos, Guarani, Calusa, Coosa, Spaniards, French, and English. When uncertain of the exact name, we chose instead to use the terms *Indian* or *European* or *African peoples.*

The use of descriptive terms does have impact on perceptions. While our languages are filled with these sensitive terms, that have been employed for centuries, it is necessary to consider the correct context in which to use the terms.

As we studied more deeply, it was evident that it was necessary to remain sensitive to the varied interpretations, understandings, and consequences of the phenomenon that we recognize as the Quincentenary of Columbus's 1492 voyage. Furthermore, we have sought to dispel myths regarding our history as people in America and the manner in which we have learned about our past.

The 500th anniversary of the meeting of two separate parts of the world provides us now the opportunity to reflect on that meeting and its significance with more circumspection. History remains not the opportunity to judge but to reach understanding. The significance of certain historical events is always subject to measure. What happened as a result of the contact of America and the Mediterranean world in the late fifteenth century is very much explained by an understanding of that period of time in its context, not as we would wish it to be. What did happen is history; it cannot be changed. History can be enlarged to encompass more of the key actors and complementary significant activities. Those of us in America are part of, and are affected deeply by, that phenomenon.

In 1992, the world has become conscious of the 500th anniversary of Columbus's first voyage to America. Emphases will vary from group to group and from continent to continent. Some of the acts of recognition will be quite agitated. However, the increased attention presents us the necessary opportunity to reexamine a number of the significant issues that are raised by this widely recognized historical event. Ultimately the commemoration of Columbus's 1492 voyage is the study of America, its people, its expanse, its place in the world, and the continuing relationship among and between peoples in the hemisphere.

INUIT

ATHABASCAN

ALGONQUIAN

BEOTHUK

HURON

Hochelaga
Onondaga

IROQUOIAN

Cahokia

CADDO

SHOSHONI

Mississippi R.

TEWA
Taos

MUSCOGEAN

Zuñi

APACHE

TIMUCUA

CHICHIMEC

CALUSA

TAINO

TARASCAN

NAHAU

AZTEC EMPIRE

CARIB

Tenochtitlan

MIXTEC

MAYA

CARIBBEAN

Atlantic
Ocean

ZAPOTEC

SEA

CHIBCHA

MUISCA

Orinoco R.

Quitu

Pacific

Amazon R.

Ocean

INCA

GÉ

EMPIRE

Cuzco

QUECHUA

Lake Titicaca

TUPIAN

AYMARA

Paraguay R.

Paraná R.

GUARANI

ARAUCANIAN

PATAGONIAN

CHAPTER TWO

THE INDIANS OF THE CENTRAL AREAS WHEN THE EUROPEANS ARRIVED

by JAMES LOCKHART

ECAUSE WE HAVE been hearing about them ever since we were in elementary school, most of us imagine that we know who the Indians are, much as we are familiar with the identity of the French or the English. Sometimes we wonder if we should call them Native Americans instead; but rarely, perhaps, does it occur to us that, aside from the exact term to be used, the very category is quite problematic. Perhaps the clearest justification for a word on the order of "English" or "French" is that a group of people call themselves that; they are aware of the other members of the group and feel a conscious solidarity with them. Nothing could be further from the situation with the "Indians" in the time before the arrival of the Europeans. No word with approximately the same scope as Indian or Native American existed in any indigenous language. The thrust of such terms is to differentiate the inhabitants of the Western Hemisphere from the rest of humanity, and since the people we call Indians were unaware of the rest, it follows that they had no need for words relating to them. But our Indians were also not fully aware of each other. Some long-distance trade networks existed, and the Incas of the central Andes created a political entity stretching far more than a thousand miles up and down the western side of South America; but no indigenous group had a clear sense of the nature and location of the majority of the others in America.

And a varied lot the peoples of the hemisphere were! North and South America between them contained hundreds of groups speaking mutually unintelligible languages. Their cultures were as separate and as different from each other as those of ancient Egypt and the Bushmen of the Kalahari Desert. America contained within itself a cultural variety fully comparable to that of Africa or Asia, and far exceeding Europe's.

We may ask then if, granting that they possessed kaleidoscopic variety and lacked a general self-consciousness, the peoples of the Western Hemisphere had anything else in common that would justify our using a name such as Indian. The answer is that they did. As different as they were, they shared a long period of isolation from the people living on the other continents; with the possible exception of the aboriginal Australians, they were the most isolated major segment of humanity. For thousands of years they had lived and evolved separately, often parallel to other peoples but not sharing directly in their achievements and hardships. One result was the lack of certain things in the Americas that existed in most of the rest of the world, giving the

Facing page: **Selected Indian groups, cultures, cities, and languages in America on the eve of European settlement. Line drawing by Stephen Kraft.**

America was home to hundreds of different Indian groups, who used numerous and variant languages.

[37]

Hammock. In Fernández de Oviedo y Valdés. *La Historia general y natural de las Indias . . .* **Seville, 1535. Rare Book and Special Collections Division.**

Gonzalo Fernández de Oviedo y Valdés (b. Madrid, 1478; d. Santo Domingo, 1557) was fifteen years old when Columbus returned to Spain after his first voyage to the "Indies." Perhaps inspired by these dramatic events, and with a growing curiosity for the nature of the newly found lands, Oviedo sailed in 1514 on the first of many journies to America, where for over thirty years he compiled detailed ethnographic descriptions of such an innumerable list of products and goods, peoples and customs that he found it "almost impossible to write [about,] given the abundance of ideas that come to mind" (*La Historia general y natural de las Indias . . .* , 1535). Thus, he painstakingly introduced Europe to an enormous variety of previously unheard of New World "exotica" such as the pineapple, the canoe, the smoking of tobacco, and the hammock. Oviedo frequently illustrated his writings with woodcut drawings because, as he wrote, "without a doubt the eyes play a great part in the information of these things, and given that they themselves cannot be seen or touched, the image of them is a great help to the pen" (*Historia . . .* , Book 5).

Preferring Castilian because of its simplicity over the more erudite Latin, he noted in Spanish, "The indians sleep in a bed they call an *hamaca* which looks like a piece of cloth with both an open and tight weave, like a net . . . made of cotton . . . about 2.5 or 3 yards long, with many henequen twine strings at either end which can be hung at any height. They are good beds, and clean . . . and since the weather is warm they require no covers at all . . . and they are portable so a child can carry it over the arm." It has been suggested that sailors no longer had to sleep on the insalubrious floors of ships during lengthy ocean crossings once the hammock had been "discovered" on the island of Hispaniola.

Along with Pedro Mártir de Anglería and Bartolomé de Las Casas, Oviedo was one of the first European "chroniclers of the Indies." He authored two comprehensive works on America: *Sumario de la natural historia de las Indias,* published in Toledo in 1526; and *La Historia general y natural de las Indias, islas y Tierra-Firme del mar Océano,* part of which was published during his lifetime, in 1535 in the city of Seville. The rare copy of *Historia . . .* signed by the author was acquired by the Library of Con-

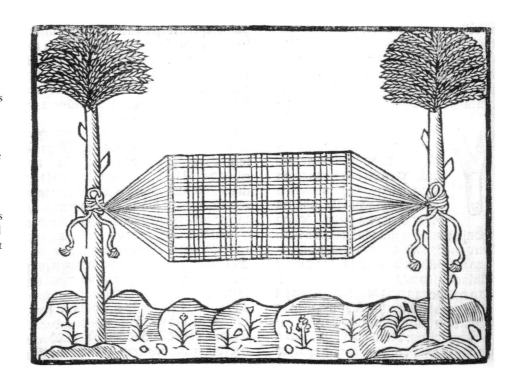

Indians a common relationship to the outsiders, once they were brought into contact with them. They all lacked immunities to disease strains that had long been passing back and forth over the contiguous landmass of Eurasia and Africa, so that all of them, whether an Inca ruler in his glittering court amid his vast warehouses and armies, or some hunter and gatherer of the plains, were susceptible to the ravages of epidemic disease whenever they came into contact with Europeans and Africans. Certain groups had made remarkable progress in metallurgy, but all the Indians lacked iron and steel, much less gunpowder, and thus none of the indigenous societies, from the most elaborately organized to the simplest, could face the Europeans on a fully equal military footing.

This shared isolation meant that all of the Indians could be conquered by European peoples once contact was made, if the outsiders found it truly worth their while, and that the waves of disease that followed upon contact greatly reduced the population everywhere, in some places eliminating it altogether. But the lack of certain metals and antibodies among the Indian peoples, which made European expansion such a different thing in America than in Africa and Asia, does not begin to tell us about the nature of the cultures.

In broad terms, the Indians were a great deal like other peoples all over the world. The most populous groups shared the most with the Europeans, and it is no accident that it was to them that the Spaniards were to be most attracted in the sixteenth century; it is to them, too, that this chapter is devoted (see Chapter 7 for more on other indigenous groups). These fully sedentary, highly organized people were located primarily up and down the central Andes and in what is now central and southern Mexico and Guatemala, a culture area we refer to as Mesoamerica. Whether we are thinking of the pre-Conquest period or the first post-Conquest centuries, we can with much justification call these two regions simply the central areas. It was here that the inhabitants of the hemisphere varied most from certain stereotypes of what an "Indian" is, which tend to characterize Indians in fluid, mobile, scattered groupings called "tribes," led by "chiefs," housed in temporary or portable structures, living to a large extent from hunting and the fruits of the land, worshiping "spirits."

Nothing could be further from the Mesoamerican or central Andean scheme of things. Here we find most of the population engaged in intensive agriculture; terracing, irrigation, and land reclamation, sometimes on a grand scale, were among the techniques in use. The same plots often remained in cultivation generation after generation. Each family worked its own land and left its holdings to the children. (In the central areas, men did the basic agricultural labor, as in Eurasia. Note in Chapter 7 that when less sedentary peoples engaged in agriculture, it was often women who did most of the work.)

Not only did the people live in sturdily built houses of wood, stone, or adobe, but they practiced a large-scale public architecture featuring massive use of cut stone. They knew cotton and other textile materials, which they not only wove into clothing for their daily wear but also used as the basis of highly ornamented luxury fabrics which were among their main forms of artistic expression. They knew how to mine and work precious metals, with which they fashioned marvelous artifacts, not to speak of their beautiful and serviceable ceramics. The Mesoamericans had writing systems, and the Andeans used a complex arrangement of knotted string, the *quipu,* for certain kinds of records and accounting.

The central peoples lived close upon each other in major, permanent concentrations, sometimes urban in appearance, though they tended to live more evenly spread across their territories than was the practice among most Europeans. Their polities were tightly organized principalities with well-defined borders and a strong dynastic rulership. The difference between commoners and lords or nobles was marked, and some areas had additional distinct strata, such as professional merchants. Commoners paid taxes and owed labor duty to the government, which could also call upon them for military service. The nobles were the leaders in war, however, just as in old-regime Europe. Religion was highly developed, with a full pantheon of gods, somewhat comparable to those of the Greeks and Romans, and a full calendar of religious festivities. These festivities and a large number of special rites were directed by a trained priesthood recruited from the nobility and associated with the state. The numerous small local kingdoms covering the area were often united in larger confederations, which sometimes reached the proportions of the empires we have all heard about.

All of the things we have been discussing had close parallels in Europe, either in its society and culture in the early modern period or in its medieval and ancient history. The parallels make understanding easier for us, as they did for Spaniards of the sixteenth century, and the implications of the similarities for what would happen after contact are enormous. Yet we need to see these civilizations on their own terms, too, or to put it another way, we need to examine also the ways in which they were different from Europe, or at least idiosyncratic. Let us be clear that the large political structures we call empires—the Inca (a name much used among the people involved) and the Aztec

gress in 1867. In his works, the naturalist states his objection to those writers who describe America from Europe, "without knowing its faces and breathing its fragrances."

Barbara M. Loste

Le Chimborazo vu depuis le Plateau de Tapia in Alexander von Humboldt and Aimé Bonpland. *Voyage de Humboldt et Bonpland . . . 1ère partie; relation historique . . .* **Paris, F. Schoell, 1810. Rare Book and Special Collections Division.**

Snow-fringed peaks, high arid plateaus, and deep luxuriant valleys all characterize one of the natural land formations most often associated with South America: the mountain system known as the *Cordillera de las Andes.* It was largely in this region of extreme and variable heights with its richly variegated fauna and flora that the Inca empire flourished at the time of the Conquest.

Chimborazo, a formidable extinct volcano of some 22,000 feet, is situated in central Ecuador. In pre-Conquest times, it was located in the northern part of the Inca empire. For a long period, it was considered the highest Andean mountain.

From 1799 to 1804, the renowned explorer and naturalist, Alexander von Humboldt, accompanied by the botanist, Aimé Bonpland, made a scientific excursion to South and Central America collecting numerous plant specimens and studying flora, fauna, and geology. In his illustrations and accompanying text, Alexander von Humboldt sought to capture and to convey the essence of the pre-Columbian world.

In Chimborazo he depicts a salient natural feature that probably looked much the same in the pre-Conquest era. The various indigenous groups living in the Andean region of the pre-Conquest period venerated numerous mountains either as sacred places or as anthropomorphic divinities. According to legend, the people of Petate and others in the area worshipped the mountain Tungurahua as a female deity and considered her either married to or the lover of Chimborazo; it was also commonly believed that the two mountains, despite their immense sizes, would visit and communicate with each other.[1] By placing Chimborazo frontally and symmetrically, Humboldt manages to endow the mountain with a majestic calm and an imposing presence worthy of divinity. In order to give the scene a greater sense of local color, Humboldt adds the figures of indigenous people on their way to market and vivid examples of animals and vegetation: the llama, the cactus, and the agave.

Humboldt's interest in Chimborazo and in tropical mountain ranges in general reflected, according to Stephen Jay Gould, his recognition "that the greatest diversity of life and terrain would be found in mountainous and tropical regions."[2] In his multivolume travel journal and other writings, Humboldt deftly fuses science and art. These works served as a source of inspiration for numerous scientists, artists, and explorers of the nineteenth century, including Darwin, Rugendas, and Church.

Anthony Páez Mullan

Notes

1. J. Jijón y Caamaño. *La Religión del Imperio de las Incas,* Vol. 1, *Los Fundamentos del Culto . . .* (Quito, 1919), p. 321.

2. Stephen Jay Gould. "Church, Humboldt, and Darwin: The Tension and Harmony of Art and Science" in *The Paintings of Frederic Edwin Church* by Franklin Kelly et al. (Washington: National Gallery of Art and Smithsonian Press, 1989), p. 97.

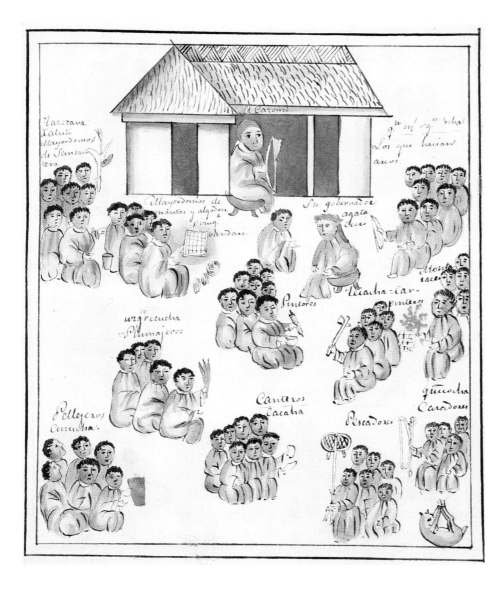

source from the Conquest period that essentially expresses an indigenous point of view. The text and numerous illustrations describe and show the organization of the Tarascan government, the duties of minor and royal household officials, and the role of a prominent group of women attached to the *Cazonci* or ruler. In addition, the *Relación* refers to various customs including visionary experiences that may be accounted for by the fairly widespread use of hallucinogenic plants.[1]

The Tarascans inhabited Michoacán, an area west of Tenochtitlán (present-day Mexico City) and south of Guadalajara. At the time of the Conquest, they were independent, although the Mexicas (Aztecs), their neighbors, had tried, on numerous occasions, to subdue them. According to the *Relación,* they were a highly stratified group with a *Cazonci*; through military prowess they had maintained their independence. Their language was not related to Nahuatl, the language of the Mexicas.

In this illustration, the unidentified artist has depicted schematically various occupational groups existing before the coming of the Spanish. Groups of seated figures are placed one above the other with little differentiation except for an object or symbol such as a net, a loom, a bow and an arrow, a writing instrument, feathers, etc., that identifies the occupation of a specific group. A couple of figures in the upper part of the illustration sit alone and are identified by glosses as being the *Cazonci* and "su gobernador" (their governor).

Stylistically this manuscript incorporates elements of both pre-Conquest manuscript painting and European pictorial tradition. In the words of Elizabeth Boone, this work primarily manifests a "flat, even-hued, static Precolumbian painting style" although the artist hints at depth in the way he arranges his groups.[2] The presence of Spanish and Tarascan terminology side by side is also a reminder of the interaction of the two cultures.

Anthony Páez Mullan

Notes

1. For a brief account of the *Relación* . . . see J. Benedict Warren. *The Conquest of Michoacán: The Spanish Domination of the Tarascan Kingdom in Western Mexico, 1521–1530* (Norman, Okla.: University of Oklahoma Press, 1985), chap. 1.

2. Elizabeth Boone. "Painted Manuscripts" in *Mexico: Splendors of Thirty Centuries* (New York: Metropolitan Museum of Art, 1990), p. 268.

Occupational Groups. Ink and wash drawing. In *Relación de las ceremonias y ritos y población y gobierno de los indios de la provincia de Mechoacán,* **compiled by Fray Jeronimo de Alcalá (?). 19th-century copy of original, ca. 1540. Peter Force Collection, Manuscript Division.**

The *Relación de las ceremonias y ritos y población y gobierno de los indios de la provincia de Michoacán* is a well-illustrated manuscript from Mexico that chronicles the history and customs of the Tarascan people before as well as during the Conquest in the area of Michoacán. This copy, one of two in the United States, is a fine nineteenth-century facsimile of the original housed in the library of El Escorial in Spain. Although the work was written by a Franciscan friar, it is largely based on the accounts of informants among the Tarascan nobility and priests—thus it is significant as a

(a name with little basis in the vocabulary of the time)—were not nations. They rested on a broad cultural similarity over an extended area, and there was some linguistic basis for them, since Nahuatl speakers like the Aztecs (Mexica would be a better term) were the most numerous group in central Mexico, and Quechua speakers were the same in the central Andes. Many languages were spoken even in the core areas, however, and even the speakers of the dominant languages failed to identify primarily with the larger language group.

Let us look at the situation in central Mexico, which we know best because of the Indian-language documents the people of that area have left us. The Nahuas, who inhabited most of the region, lived in some hundreds of small ethnic states, with anywhere from a couple of thousand to fifty or even a hundred thousand inhabitants in each. Such a state was called an *altepetl* (meaning literally "water and mountain," in reference to the people's territory). What we call the Aztec Empire was a confederation of three *altepetl,* of which the leading and largest was México Tenochtitlán, on the site of present-day Mexico City. By virtue of a series of conquests they carried out, these three states collected tributes of all kinds from many of the other *altepetl* of the region, and arranged interdynastic marriages with them to their own advantage. In this way they succeeded in building a strong power base, attracting many people to themselves, and unifying the regional economy to a large extent.

But the people of the whole region did not become Mexica (the name for the inhabitants of Tenochtitlán). Some large states, like the four-part confederation of Tlaxcala, were entirely outside the Mexica network. And even in the area of Mexica dominance, each group still lived within its own separate *altepetl,* which kept its name, its people, usually most of its territory, and a ruler from its own dynasty. When the kingdom of Xochimilco, say, was conquered by the Mexica and their allies, the people remained the Xochimilca, proudly distinct from all outsiders, be they Mexica or citizens of other *altepetl.* Each *altepetl* had its own origin legend going back to the creation of the universe, and though the legends look a great deal alike from afar, each group was convinced that it was the true protagonist of the story. Each had, in addition to its own king, its own market and its own special god, who was often a mixture of a god from the general pantheon and a deified ancestor from the legend of origin.

Nor did the feeling of separateness stop there. Each *altepetl* consisted of a number of smaller units, *calpulli,* which were microcosms of it, with a smaller version of all its institutions: a lord, a market, a deity, even a special version of the origin legend, assigning a central role to that particular entity and casting doubt on the contributions of its fellows. The overall result was an extremely varied cultural and ethnic mosaic. Larger political units often formed under military pressure, and also in response to the deeper need for order and economic unity across a broader region of basically similar culture; such agglomerations might have splendid success and last for some generations, but they never transcended a fierce general microethnicity.

Political life is in fact an excellent illustration of a prime tendency of Nahua civilization (and many other indigenous cultures as well, it seems): the creation of larger units of any kind through symmetrical, often numerical arrangements of smaller parts that remain quite distinct from each other,

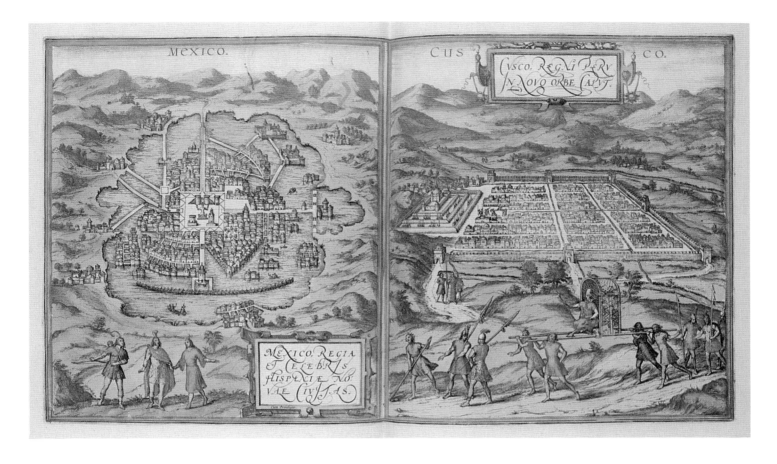

functioning through rotation or allocation within the larger framework. The parts of the local state, the *altepetl,* were the various *calpulli,* often eight of them (the Nahuas tended to divide things into twos, fours, and eights). Each would take turns, in a fixed order, in doing labor duty for the ruler of the *altepetl* throughout the year; each would have its tribute allotment to the larger entity; each would have its space and its specialty in the *altepetl* marketplace; each would contribute its own contingent in time of war. Thus the *altepetl* could function in an orderly way, and yet the individuality and autonomy of the *calpulli* could be expressed. When the Nahuas created macrounits, they used the same principle. The large confederation of Tlaxcala consisted of four *altepetl;* the triple alliance that we call the Aztec empire consisted of three.

Subdivision did not stop with the *calpulli.* In each there were a set of wards—collections of households—which took turns at that level and maintained a certain separateness. Life in the household itself operated on similar principles. It was a single unit toward the outside, for the people lived in a complex inside a single enclosure and had a single obligation to pay tribute in labor and in kind. Within the complex, though, stood separate buildings where each couple or nuclear family lived, each with its own storage space. And just so the lands that the household group held were divided—often scattered in different places, but in any case usually worked separately by the different members. In some places the Nahuas cultivated great stretches of land, but they always consisted, in principle, of a series of small uniform plots.

Tenochtitlán and Cuzco. In Georg Braun and Francis Hogenberg. *Civitates Orbis Terrarum.* Cologne, 1612–18. Geography and Map Division.

The principal centers of the Mexica (Aztec) and Inca empires were the great cities of Tenochtitlán and Cuzco. There are no adequate words to express the feelings of Cortés's soldiers as they looked down into Tenochtitlán in 1519, where they saw an active city of ca. 300,000 with a thriving market place, a zoo, an aviary, temples and other huge buildings, and a lake choked with boats engaged in the conduct of all types of commerce. Cuzco was an extraordinary city to the Spaniards. Pedro Sancho, who arrived there in November 1533, remarked, "It is so beautiful and large that it would be something to see in Spain." Cuzco was a city with a population between 100,000 and 200,000 persons, situated some 9,900 feet above sea level.

Origins of the Mexican peoples. In Fray Diego Durán. *La Historia antigua de la Nueva España.* **Manuscript facsimile, ca. 19th century [original 1585]. Peter Force Collection, Manuscript Division.**

Durán's manuscript is in three sections, each illustrated by drawings having diverse origins and remote inspiration in native traditions. According to legend the Mexica (Aztec) people came from a place called Aztlán, probably in the southwest part of the present-day United States.

We find the same thing in artistic expression. Temple complexes consisted of separate similar units, each with projecting serpent heads or other emblems distributed in a pattern across the surface and decorative panels on which jaguars, wolves, or eagles repeated in twos, fours, or eights. In painting, depictions of gods, animals, or plants consisted of various detachable parts, each marked off from the others. Nahua songs illustrate the principle superbly. The ones preserved never tell a story or present a linear argument, but hover about a common theme. The unit of which they are built is a verse that never overtly refers to any other in the song; two verses, sharing some of the same material in the manner of a refrain, make a pair, and a song consists of a certain number of pairs of verses, most often four, making the usual eight. Here is a verse pair, with the nonsense syllables that mark the end of each verse:

> Flower-feathered is the bird who delights, delights himself above the
>   flowers. *A ohuaya ohuaya.*
> Sipping at various blooms he delights, delights himself above the
>   flowers. *A ohuaya ohuaya.*

Nahua histories worked along somewhat the same lines, though less rigidly symmetrical. Everything was organized by year. Events were simply inserted in order of occurrence under a certain year. The four repeated year signs (reed, flint knife, house, rabbit) and the cycle of thirteen numbers, rotating jointly to make a fifty-two-year "century," formed a framework much like the numbered verses of the songs.

The universe was no different. The Nahuas placed great emphasis on the four cardinal directions, the same ones familiar to us; but to them the number four had a greater significance. And the directions were in a fixed sequence,

Coronation of Montezuma. In Fray Diego Durán. *La Historia antigua de la Nueva España.* **Manuscript facsimile, ca. 19th century [original 1585]. Peter Force Collection, Manuscript Division.**

Following the reign of Ahuitzotl (1486–1502), Montezuma was king of the Mexicas until he was killed in 1520. It is he who foresaw the arrival of newcomers from the east (the Spaniards); his successor, Cuauhtemoc, ruled during the period of the Spanish Conquest.

east to north to west to south, making a rotational scheme much like the *altepetl.* Indeed, the similarity was not lost on the Nahuas. The directional rotation was subdivided so that each political subunit had its particular spot, and this was then associated with a particular time of the year, so that religious and other duties fell due at that time. Thus time and space fell together, as they do in theories of physics, and political organization reflected the cosmos.

Time too was to be divided into four. In Nahua cosmology, there had been four ages before ours, four progressively more successful attempts by the gods to create something like humans, each ending in a catastrophe setting it off from the others. That our age is the fifth is not merely an anomaly. The Nahuas often imagined their favorite fours set off by a fifth number that in a way summarized and symbolized the set of four. It is so that they conceived their vigesimal system (that is, based on twenty)—four sets of fives, each four with its culminator that makes it five. The Nahua "month" was twenty days: four sets of four plus days named for the four year signs dominating each set. Two kinds of years were counted simultaneously, one a solar year of eighteen twenty-day months and the other a ritual calendar of thirteen such months, used especially for divination. With so many interlocking, rotating schemes, using the same elements at different levels, it was natural that the Nahuas, like all the other Mesoamericans, saw equivalences in everything and tended to think of time itself as cyclical. A person or an event was easily seen as a repetition from an earlier generation, or something that might repeat in the future. Yet in its complexity, the Mesoamerican system also allowed for the linear march of the years over centuries and millennia.

Let us skip past the famous Mayans, who as Mesoamericans shared a great deal with the Nahuas (though they were no longer flourishing in quite the same way as earlier when the Spaniards arrived), and see if we can detect similarities in the Andean world. The relative lack of sources written by the Andeans in their own language keeps us from penetrating deeply into many of the concepts by which they organized their lives. But similarities can in fact be found.

The Inca empire spread over a vaster area and included a larger proportion of the inhabitants of that area than anything similar in Mesoamerica. It also operated in ways either unique to the Andes or on a much larger scale than anywhere else—it built impressive roads tying the region together, developed a system of entrepôts and warehouses, systematically moved people about for its own purposes, extracted large numbers of young women from the general population to serve the empire in weaving, religious duties, and other ways, and organized vast labor drafts and armies encompassing the whole domain, sometimes in connection with extensive irrigation and terracing projects.

But when we look closer, we find much that is familiar from Mesoamerica. The Incas were based in Cuzco as the Mexica were based in México Tenochtitlán. Not all the inhabitants of the Andes were considered Incas. Local kingdoms that the Incas conquered continued to exist as such, with their own rulership, their own borders, and usually their own language. Rebellions and schisms were rife. What the Incas essentially did was to establish an impressive network outside the local kingdoms, utilizing their resources in a larger framework but leaving them standing. Although we know relatively little about the organization of such kingdoms, we can say that like their Mesoamerican counterparts they had a strong ethnic, cultural, and linguistic base, each imagining itself a separate people with a distinct origin, and they were built up out of constituent parts very much like the *calpulli* of the Nahuas. The cellular unit in the Andes was called an *ayllu*. As among the Nahuas, it had its own territory, its own deified ancestors, and its own internal economy and society; it appears to have been more kin-oriented and closed to the outside than its central Mexican equivalent. And as with the Nahuas again, units were arranged in twos, fours, and other schemes. The Incas conceived their empire as divided into four sectors. Cuzco itself was mentally organized as a great circle divided into several parts by lines radiating from a center past certain holy places. The parts so defined rotated in the religious calendar and apparently in carrying out many other functions.

One of the implications of cellular organization that comes through more strongly in the Andes than in Mesoamerica is reciprocity (not that it was unimportant in Mesoamerica). The word for the general rotating labor obligation that was so central to Andean achievements was *mita,* meaning "turn," "season," and the like. Each person and each unit was to make a contribution to the commonwealth and receive something in recompense. When workers did *mita* duty for the lords or the priests, they received provisions, clothing, or other gifts in return, often in organized festivities which brought the divine into the system as well. The rulers' reciprocal contributions may have been primarily symbolic, but reciprocity itself was central to the whole Andean way of life. By present understanding, the central Andes lacked the well-developed marketplaces of Mesoamerica, relying instead on reciprocal redistribution to allocate needed goods and services across the region.

Such a way of doing things was greatly furthered by the unusual Andean geography. The region is close to the equator but not uniformly hot because

Facing page:
Calendar Wheel. In Mariano Fernández de Echeverría y Veytia. *Historia del orígen de las gentes que poblaron la America septentrional* [early 19th-century manuscript facsimile]. Peter Force Collection, Manuscript Division.

The *tonalpohualli,* or sacred calendar, ruled the life of each Mexica and was consulted on all important occasions. It was made up of 260 days, or 20 months of 13 days.

[46]

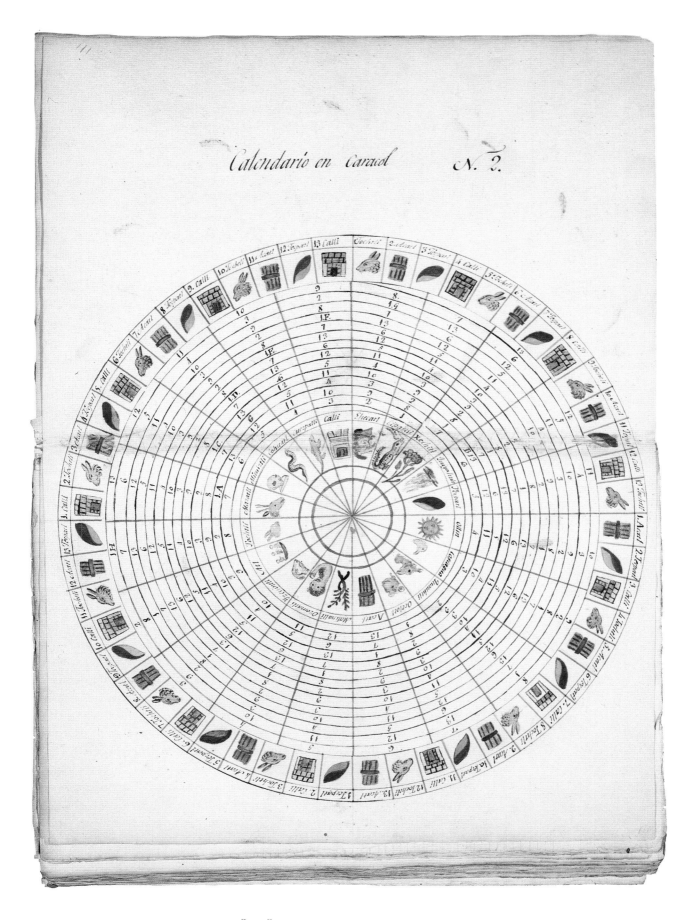

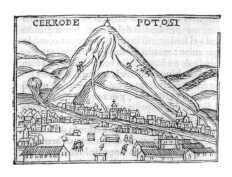

Potosí. In Agustín de Zarate. *Historia del descubrimiento y conquista del Perú.* **Anvers, 1555. Rare Book and Special Collections Division.**

Potosí, an Andean city that existed before the rise of the Incan empire and an active one during the period of that empire, was of profound interest to the Spaniards. The city was looked upon as a mountain of silver that could be used to fuel future Spanish expansion. Its existence captivated the minds of Europeans who sought ways to reach the resource for their own benefit.

of huge altitude differences within very short distances. Volcanic peaks may be covered with snow while beneath them stretch areas of high cold plain producing grass good for the native llamas and alpacas; lower (but still cold) lands produce potatoes and other Andean tubers; below that, temperate areas support maize; wet slopes of the lower hills are propitious for coca, much used as a narcotic and for offerings; and finally come hot river valleys close to sea level, producing a variety of tropical specialties. Andean culture drew on the products of all these zones. Rather than lowland kingdoms trading in local specialities with highland kingdoms, the archetypal picture in the Andes was a kingdom that had lands in each of the many zones and supplied itself. A sociopolitical group in the Andes, though tightly organized, might be dispersed over a large area; its parts would not by any means always be contiguous, and its people would move about a great deal, going from one section to another. Segments of a given locality might belong to several different sets of people, each with different affiliations.

Mesoamerican numerical symmetry began with duality; in the Andes, duality is even more pronounced. Many Mesoamerican kingdoms were divided into distinct halves, but in the Andes this was a normal, expected feature, strongly emphasized in the political ideology. Almost any larger unit (Cuzco included) would have an upper and a lower half, each with its own leader, functioning in many ways as an independent entity, though always rotating and reciprocating with its partner. These halves were part of a duality that existed at many levels, helping importantly in the mental integration of Andean life.

The upper half and the lower half were associated with a whole set of parallel contrasts running through Andean culture: sun and moon; male and female; land and water; outsider and insider. As in most cultures until recently, gender roles were rigid and well defined. In the Andes, gender was perhaps especially well incorporated into the world view. The basic aspects of the natural world, the divine, and human culture were identified as either male or female, making a scheme of complementary pairs. Descent was reckoned in two columns, the females coming down from the women of the family and the males from the men. The upper half of a kingdom was schematically male, the lower female. One can see that under these circumstances notions of "upper" and "lower," "male" and "female," broadened far beyond the meanings we usually give them to become part of a rich symbolic tapestry.

The high cultures of the Western Hemisphere gave a larger role to the spoken word than we do today, and this is true even of the Mesoamericans, despite their systems of writing. It is true that several centuries before the arrival of the Spaniards, the lowland Maya had evolved methods of turning whole sentences into a written form, with precise indication of parts of speech and inflections, and they often used their skills in inscriptions on public buildings and in codices. Recently, exciting advances have been made in deciphering texts of this type. They turn out, however, to be quite limited in scope, mainly referring to the bare bones of dynastic history and celebratory ritual. Even this art seems to have declined considerably by the sixteenth century.

As for the Nahuas of central Mexico, they did a great deal of writing, or what we would call writing, but their system was even farther from capturing large stretches of running prose than that of the ancient Maya. Their numer-

Idol at Copán. In Frederick Cather-wood. Detail. *Views of Ancient Monuments in Central America, Chiapas, and Yucatan.* **New York, 1844. Rare Book and Special Collections Division.**

The rich architecture and writing of the Mayan peoples of Central America and Mexico were captured in the nineteenth-century lithographic prints of John Stephens and Frederick Catherwood, who visited the sites. Mayan culture rivaled that of the Incas and Mexicas (Aztecs); however, its period of prominence predated late fifteenth-century contact with Europe.

El Tajín Temple, Veracruz, Mexico. Photo.

This Totonac capital on the Gulf Coast of Mexico endured as a center from the fifth to the thirteenth centuries. It occupied an extensive area of rolling hills over which numerous structural groups were scattered. The Pyramid of the Niches represents a high point in Totonac architecture and is one of the most outstanding examples of religious construction among Mesoamerican Indian cultures. The most popular pre-Columbian ball game was played on courts in El Tajín.

als and calendrical signs were sophisticated, and they could and did represent the names of people and places through pictures of the things designated by the elements in the name; thus the kingdom of Azcapotzalco, which literally means "anthill," would be shown as an ant and a mound, somewhat conventionalized. Other glyphs, also originally pictures but much transformed by convention, represented some important words such as "sun," "water," "rock," and "mountain." With these tools, the Nahuas kept efficient records concerning matters like the calendar, tribute payment, and land tenure.

Most matters were put only partly on paper. To take one important example, already alluded to above, the Nahuas were very concerned with the history of their kingdoms, which they recorded in works we can call annals, since they are organized solely by calendar year. Each event—the succession of a king, a plague of locusts, a legendary foundation—would typically be represented by only one more or less elaborate pictorial ensemble containing some glyphs giving the key elements. The rest, the narrative proper, had to be reconstructed orally from the memory of the writer and custodian of the document. Thus far more was in the mind of the "reader" than was depicted visually. It was a two-track system of communication that one might compare to television or to a slide lecture. Indeed, the Nahuas did not conceive of writing as a separate category, as we do. They made no distinction between what we would call writing and what we would call painting, but used the equivalent of "painting" for both. Their way of looking at it was particularly appropriate because their painting was less realistic and more conventional than most of ours, taking on more of a symbolic nature and requiring something like reading.

At any rate, the Nahua system left more of a role for conversation, speechmaking, and other oral forms than we are accustomed to. The songs mentioned above were not written down at all. Much of the lore of society was carried in formulaic speech, easily memorized and repeated on many occasions. As part of this oral formula, many Nahuatl expressions were double: "blouse and skirt" meant "woman"; "the tail and the wing," the common people; "one with eyes and ears," an alert, astute person. The word for the local state, the *altepetl,* which as we saw meant literally "water and mountain," is another of these. The Nahuas were very preachy and given to flights of oratorical rhetoric. No occasion was without its set speech: weddings, births, accessions of kings, going on trips and returning from them, even getting up in the morning and eating ordinary meals. Most such speeches had the flavor of advice, and they were often uttered by the elder to the younger, giving rise to a whole genre called *huehuetlatolli,* "the ancient words" (or possibly "the words of the elderly"), in which the received tradition is passed on to the next generation, and at the same time the arts of polite speech and good etiquette are taught. Those arts were not simple. An elaborate protocol saw that respect for everyone was maintained but at the same time everyone was ranked relative to everyone else. In a refined network of veiled meanings, kinship terms were inverted; a king would call his aides his grandfathers, and the aides would call the king their grandchild.

In the Andes, we can surmise that oral culture had much the same nature, all the more so because visual communication was even less systematized, although we lack many of the spoken texts themselves. We do know, for example, that kinship terms in extended meanings were even more woven

**Fragment. From the *Codex Dresdensis*
[Dresden Codex] in Sachsische Landes-
bibliothek, Dresden. Facsimile [Aka-
demische Druck und Verlagsanstalt,
Graz, 1990] of the original, ca. 13th
century. Rare Book and Special Collections Division.**

The oldest known Mayan codex, the Dresden Codex, dates from the beginning of the
thirteenth century. It is a treatise on divination and astronomy. The Mesoamerican codices, of which the Mayan are a part, are
the best source of information about the inhabitants of pre-Columbian America. Only
a few survived the Conquest and time.
Mayan writing used pictography, ideograms,
logograms, syllables, and signs representing
forms.

into society and polity in the Andes than in central Mexico.

All these things we have been discussing are an important part of the
identity and individuality of the Andean and Mesoamerican peoples. They
are not, of course, entirely unique in kind. Europeans too had various rotational schemes, and though they wrote much down, they also made great use
of orality and rhetoric. The Spaniards especially were much inclined to a
proud localism and regional strife that had much in common with the microethnicity of the New World inhabitants. It is true, on the other hand, that
some features of New World culture can be seen as primarily in contrast to
that of Europe, and have been so seen from the time of first contact until
today. The most notable of these is the practice of human sacrifice, which the
Europeans had many centuries behind them and with which they could not
identify—an attitude most of us continue to have today. Human sacrifice was
a standard feature of the culture of both the Andes and Mesoamerica; in the
latter it was more highly developed, and among the Nahuas of central Mexico
it reached a climax in the years immediately before contact. At the level of
ideology, it was part of the New World reciprocity between the divine and
the human; at the political level, it served the interests of ethnic states, and
in its late central Mexican form it was used to impress other states with Mexica power. It thus fits into the general picture in several ways; but let us
remember that it is only a small part of that picture.

Overall, the peoples of the great central areas had a large number of
points of contact with the Europeans of the fifteenth and sixteenth centuries.
On confrontation with each other, both sides would see a great deal that they
would immediately recognize. Sometimes a deep, true similarity of form and
function existed, as with the Spanish and the Mesoamerican notions of nobility; in other cases the apparent similarity was more superficial, as with some
elements of religious doctrine. In almost every aspect of life, interaction was
possible, and the outlook for cultural survivals from the pre-Conquest period,
at least through a long transitional period, was propitious.

ATLANTIC OCEAN

AZORES

MADEIRA ISLANDS

CANARY ISLANDS

PORTUGAL

Valladolid
Bordeaux
NAVARRE
Segovia
ARAGON
Marseille
Lisbon
Toledo
TAGUS R.
Barcelona
Valencia
Seville
CASTILE
Palos
Granada
Cadiz
Tangier
Fez
Algiers
Tunis

Marrakech

AFRICA

Milan
Vienna
Genoa
Venice
Florence
Rome
DANUBE R.
OTTOMAN
Salonika
BLACK SEA
Caffa
Constantinople
EMPIRE
SARDINIA
MEDITERRANEAN SEA
SICILY
CRETE
Antioch
Tripoli
Barka
Alexandria
Jerusalem
Cairo
NILE R.
RE...

The Mediterranean World in 1492. Line drawing by Stephen Kraft.

The Mediterranean—the "Sea in the Middle of the Earth"—links the peoples of Europe, Africa, and Asia.

CHAPTER THREE

LIFE IN THE
MEDITERRANEAN WORLD

by JOHN FLEMING

HE APPARENTLY UNIVERSAL habit of the human mind, when faced with the unfamiliar and the unknown, is to attempt to accommodate it, often only by mental duress, within the categories of the familiar and the known. When in the autumn of 1492 a group of Spanish sailors on the one hand and a group of Arawak islanders on the other gazed in wonderment upon each other across the water, what they saw and how they reacted to what they saw was limited by what their respective cultures allowed them to see and do. From the European point of view this was a moment of discovery of a literally new world—a world which existed on no European map, had no European name, existed in no European mind or memory. Yet Europeans were slow to grasp the utter newness of their experience, and indeed strove to deny it. Columbus so wanted to believe that he had found a new path to the back side of an old and known place, namely Asia, that he spent month after month in the Caribbean searching for Kublai Khan. We shall never know, except by the most tenuous surmises drawn from anthropological analogies, what the Arawaks saw and thought, but they too faced an utter newness for which no previous cultural experience could possibly have prepared them.

It is not easy in brief compass and with broad brush strokes to identify even the most salient features of the two worlds that encountered each other in 1492. Each was a complex world of many tongues and kingdoms, and each was informed by powerful and diverse historical, literary, and religious traditions. Another chapter of this catalog presents a picture of native American civilizations in the age of the encounter. The task of this chapter is to identify some of the complex features of the civilization which had nourished Christopher Columbus, his patrons and collaborators, and the sailors, adventurers, brigands, businessmen, friars, and farmers who very soon followed in Columbus's wake to the Americas.

In Columbus's day the European nation states with which we are familiar had not yet come into being, and although regional and local political arrangements were of great importance, we may usefully search for Columbus's cultural formation within an international and indeed multicultural Mediterranean world. The very name of the Mediterranean Ocean, which means "the Middle of the Earth," suggests the ancient world view that still held sway over the European mind in the late fifteenth century. When men and women spoke of the sea, what they generally meant was the Mediterra-

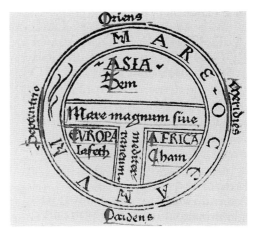

T-O Map. In Saint Isidorus [Bp. of Seville] *Etymologiarum sive originum libri xx.* **Augsburg, Gunther Zainer, 1472. Voll. Coll., Rare Book and Special Collections Division.**

The T-O map shown here represents one of the earliest examples of medieval *mappae mundi.* Originally drawn between 622 and 633 as an illustration for Isidore, Bishop of Seville's *Etymologiarum sive originum libri xx,* the most famous of his thirty encyclopedias and historical works, this map has the distinction of being the first printed world map, appearing in the 1472 printing of *Etymologiarum* produced by Gunther Zainer in Augsburg. Although the earliest extant manuscript copy of the map dates from the eighth century, it is assumed earlier manuscripts contained the same tripartite scheme. Dividing the world into the three known continents (Europe, Africa, and Asia), this scheme used the T to represent, horizontally, the Don and the Nile (or possibly the Red Sea), the traditional separation of Europe and Africa from Asia, and vertically, the Mediterranean Sea, giving it an easterly orientation. The T also represented the "tau cross," a mystical Christian symbol placing Jerusalem, their "center of the world," at the intersection of the horizontal and vertical section. The O encircling the T portrayed the common ancient and medieval idea of a world surrounded by water.

As a product of the Christian church, the T-O map's primary purpose was to support and promote the Christian world view with little importance given to geographical accuracy. With no secular world maps surviving from the Middle Ages, although a few references to such exist, it is believed that the majority of the cartographic endeavors during those years were monastic. Used to illustrate theologic texts, the earliest T-O maps, like Isidore's, were small and very simplistic in form and content. The later Middle Ages saw the production of much larger, more elaborate T-O *mappae mundi* incorporating an undifferentiated mixture of contemporary geography, historic Christianity, legend, and folklore, with modern travel narratives, both real and imagined.

With the advent of the printing press, the classic texts of past centuries, including Isidore's, were reproduced, thereby prolonging their circulation and influence beyond the late Middle Ages. In the transitional years before Columbus's first voyage, it was not unusual to find all types of *mappae mundi* coexisting with the more realistic and practical portolan chart and the scientific work of Ptolemy. The world, indeed, was ready for and in need of the tumultuous changes on the horizon.

Kathryn L. Engstrom

Zodiac. In Battista Agnese. [*Portolan Atlas*] Venice, ca. 1544. Vellum Chart Collection, Geography and Map Division. (See also pages 2 and 83.)

The zodiacal sign was one of the devices used by medieval astronomers and navigators to calculate predicted locations. The zodiac itself is an artificial belt on the celestial sphere extending 8 degrees on either side of the ecliptic, arbitrarily subdivided into twelve equal sections, 30 degrees long, which bear the names of the zodiacal constellations. These sections, or signs, are traversed successively by the sun in its apparent annual motion. The moon and planets, except for Pluto, never stray more than 8 degrees from the ecliptic. The introduction of astronomy and the calendar to European sailors by the fifteenth century became necessary for navigational purposes, as their known world was rapidly expanding, and voyages lengthened.

nean, comprehensively understood as the sum of all its parts—the Aegean, the Adriatic, the Levantine, and the Barbary Coast—and which from timeless generations had lapped against their sunny shores, from which a seemingly inexhaustible bounty of seafood had always been harvested, and across which ships had always carried rich loads of oil and wine and wool for commercial trade, or armed warriors for conquest and destruction. The ancient epic poems of the Greeks and Romans told the stories of how Greeks had once, in vengeance for the abduction of the most beautiful woman in the world, crossed the sea to make ten years of war against Troy, and how a tiny, proud band of the Trojan survivors had then crossed the sea in the opposite direction to become the founders of mighty Rome itself. If in the ancient world great empires had risen on the shores of the Mediterranean, in Columbus's time—a period that historians call late medieval, the Renaissance, or early modern according to their differing tendencies—the political states of the Mediterranean continued in their cultural, political, and material preeminence, the possessors of the richest and most agriculturally productive lands, the most populous and prosperous cities, and, it goes without saying, the centers of the greatest maritime activity.

Their known world, comprising the three continents of Europe, Asia, and Africa, surrounded the sea on all sides. The Mediterranean linked peoples of many languages and of different religions: Berbers, Blackamoors, Iberian Jews, Provençal fishermen, Genoese traders, Byzantine monks, Turks, Arabs,

and Syrians. At the extreme west, at what is now the Rock of Gibraltar and what was then the Pillars of Hercules, a narrow channel opened into the vastness of the Ocean Sea—what we now call the Atlantic. In the *Divine Comedy* of Dante, the great fourteenth-century Florentine poet, the shade of Ulysses, the sailor-hero of the ancient epic of Homer, relates how God had punished him to eternal damnation for the vice of an immoderate curiosity that enticed him to sail deep into the unknown waters of the Ocean Sea.

If the Mediterranean world exhibited a polyglot diversity, it also implied, looked at from the point of view of western Christians, a remarkable unity. In the approximate center of the sea was the city of Rome, the ancient seat of the Roman Empire and of its medieval spiritual heir, the Roman Catholic Church. In its quintessentially Christian culture, and in the Latin language, the common tongue of Catholic liturgy, the Bible, and all learned writing, Europeans found the transcendent unity that, at least in theory, could overcome their actual cultural and political divisions. In this respect Rome, center of the Mediterranean world, was more important for allegorical than for geopolitical reasons. Christianity had been born within the Roman Empire at the zenith of its power. As that empire lay in collapse in the fifth century, St. Augustine, perhaps the most authoritative of all Christian writers, had in his *City of God* reinterpreted the idea of Rome in spiritual terms. Here was the birth of the idea of Christendom, an idea that maintained the inseparable unity of citizenship with religious faith.

The correspondence of the reality to the theoretical model was, as usual, tenuous; but it was an age in which, even more markedly than in our own, invisible myth often took precedence over visible actuality. Even so, late-fifteenth-century Christendom faced a crisis that was visible to all but the willfully blind, and that was the dynamic expansion of Islam in the area of the northeastern Mediterranean. This episode of Muslim expansionism was only the latest in a series that by Columbus's time stretched back over 700 years. The idea of a hegemonous Latin Christendom coterminous with the vast lands of the Roman Empire hardly outlived Augustine himself. In the early centuries of the Middle Ages nascent Islam had conquered nearly the entire southern coastline of the Mediterranean. In the eighth century Muslim Africans had overrun all of Iberia and crossed the Pyrenees before finally being checked by Christian armies in central France. In later centuries the Islamic conquest of areas formerly Christian led to the Crusades of the high Middle Ages. The Crusades will be judged more or less successful depending upon one's point of view, but they at least demonstrated the ability of Christendom to take effective unified action far from the center of Europe. The fifteenth century, on the other hand, witnessed steady and incrementally devastating attacks on the Eastern Christian nations, and on the Christian navies in the eastern Mediterranean, by the Muslim Turks. In Western Europe Turkish expansion naturally made its most profound impact on those maritime states, like Venice and Genoa, which lived from the sea. Columbus was probably just a toddler when the Turks captured Constantinople (Istanbul) in 1453, an event considered literally apocalyptic by many fearful Christian observers.

There was one Mediterranean area of prominently visible exception to the general defensive somberness just described: the Iberian peninsula. The fifteenth century was a period of almost unqualified and triumphant glory for

The zodiac displayed here enhances the beautiful portolan atlas on vellum (ca. 1544) prepared by the Genoese mapmaker Battista Agnese, who flourished from 1536 to 1564. We know little about this early Age of Exploration cartographer beyond that which he revealed on his maps. He was born in Genoa and worked in Venice. Nearly sixty books of maps attributed to him have been identified, each containing about ten charts. The lack of substantial information about Agnese is all the more remarkable since he was recognized as one of the most prolific mapmakers of the sixteenth century. See especially Henry R. Wagner's definitive study, "The Manuscript Atlases of Battista Agnese," *Papers* (Bibliographical Society of America) 25 (1931): 1–110.

It is apparent that Agnese's atlases were never intended for use in actual navigation. Instead, he produced these maps for wealthy collectors. A practical sea pilot of that time was generally provided with only those charts that were necessary for his specific voyage. The nautical charts that Agnese compiled on vellum were based on the portolan charts. Although not a maker of original maps, Agnese was a brilliant copyist. His works were derived from a map of the world from the Sevillian chart makers, either the Diego Ribero planisphere of 1529 or one like it. By that year, the explorations of the northeast coast of America, in the Gulf of Mexico, and along both sides of Central America had been concluded. The Portuguese explorations on the coast of Brazil and those of the Spaniards in the La Plata region, the Strait of Magellan, and the north coast of South America had also been completed.

This rare Agnese manuscript atlas, acquired by the Library of Congress in 1943, was made for Heronimous Ruffault, the Abbot of St. Vedasti and St. Adriani in France. It contains fifteen vellum leaves, which include ten colorfully illuminated hand-drawn maps. Among the plates are found a double-page zodiac and maps of the Pacific, Atlantic, and the Indian Oceans, the Mediterranean and Black Seas, and an oval world map on which Magellan's route for the circumnavigation of the world is given. America appears on three of the charts. Especially noteworthy areas, such as Mexico, Yucatan (still shown as an island), and the legendary golden mountains of Peru, are colored gold for emphasis. On the back cover there is a compass surrounded by a wind rose.

The oval world map, attractively colored

in red, green, blue, and gold, generalizes the Atlantic coast of the present-day United States and the Pacific coast adjacent to southern California with an accuracy creditable only half a century after 1492. North America appears without designation; South America is designated *mundus novus*, New World. Although Agnese never visited America, he probably knew more about its geography than did the navigators who had visited its coasts and mapped small portions of them.

John R. Hébert

Lusitanus [Old Portuguese Man]. Engraving. *Omnium fere Gentium.* **Antverpiae [Antwerp], 1572. Rare Book and Special Collections Division.**

An old Iberian man is one of several illustrations of peoples and customs of all nations in this 1572 classic work.

what are the modern countries of Spain and Portugal. The prevailing mood in both places was one of buoyant optimism, nationalistic fulfillment, and religious destiny. Indeed Columbus's chief difficulties in finding backing in Portugal and Spain arose from the fact that the monarchs in both places were already so deeply preoccupied by dynamic and successful programs of expansion. The anomalous geographical position of Portugal within the Mediterranean world posed for that country special challenges but also special opportunities. Linked by language and long custom to the Romance nations to its east, it found itself drawn by its westward, Atlantic prospect to look also toward the European states of the north; and we find Portugal closely allied with England in the fourteenth century. We see how close were the medieval and the Renaissance worlds when we realize that Henry the Navigator was the grandson of the English duchess for whom the young Geoffrey Chaucer had written his first major poem. The logic of geography also determined that the Portuguese would be pioneers in the exploration of the West African coastline and its related islands. At a time in the early fifteenth century when Christians were recoiling in humiliated defeat in the eastern Mediterranean, the Portuguese launched an aggressive war that captured the North African city of Ceuta.

What was true of Portugal was truer still of those lands, today called Spain, which were finding their full cultural and political unity only under Fernando and Isabel. Much of Spain was under Islamic control during most of the Middle Ages; and while the Christian Schoolmen were debating at the University of Paris in the thirteenth century, a great Islamic culture, famous for the wealth and magnificence of its cities, was flourishing in the kingdom of Granada in southern Iberia. The culture of Islamic Spain was not merely splendid; it was also cosmopolitan. Spain, in addition to being the home of the Christians and the Moors, was also the domicile of the largest Jewish population of the diaspora, a cohesive ethnic subculture of great economic and commercial importance characterized by a vibrant spiritual and literary life.

This cosmopolitan moment was to come to its tragic end even as Columbus was raising his sails for his first voyage to America. Medieval Spanish history is in large measure the history of the gradual, unifying reconquest of Muslim Europe by the Christian duchies of northeastern and central Iberia—Catalonia, Aragon, Navarre, Valencia, and the Castilles. Its decisive phase was precisely the fifteenth century; and its decisive national character was the adversarial experience of military and religious conflict with Islam. The legendary epic hero of Christian Spain was El Cid, who warred against the turbaned armies of the caliph. The patron saint of Spain was the bellicose Apostle James, Santiago, actually called the "Moor-Slayer," who was supposed to have appeared riding through the sky on a white horse to lead the Catholic armies to victory—as he would one day be seen in central Mexico, fighting with Cortés's men against the Aztecs.

The unique features of the Spanish historical experience created a distinctive and in some ways seemingly anachronistic national character, a kind of institutionalized "crusader's mentality" founded in an intolerant and triumphalist Christian faith and expressed in terms of the militant chivalry of a warrior caste. At a time when much of the rest of Europe withdrew in literal or metaphorical retreat before the Ottomans in the East, Spain alone of the

A single leaf from the Book of Job in the Gutenberg Bible. Mainz, ca. 1454–55.

The Gutenberg Bible was the first substantial printed book in the western world. This printed Bible (containing the Vulgate text) was in production at least by 1454 and is commonly attributed to Johann Gutenberg (1400–1486) of Mainz, Germany. To its namesake belongs the credit for inventing the process of making movable metal type. Furthermore, he and his associates brought together the right combination of materials for printing and distributing a complete book.

The Gutenberg Bible stands as one of the landmarks in the history of civilization. Gutenberg's invention made it possible for humankind to record and disseminate the collected learning, art, and history of the human race in a form that was accessible to anyone who knew how to read. Before the invention of printing, human knowledge and lore were recorded and preserved in manuscripts, laboriously written by scribes in few copies that were largely inaccessible.

Scholars estimate that about two hundred copies of the Gutenberg Bible were printed. Today forty-seven copies, in various degrees of completeness, are known to exist. Most copies were printed on paper, but a small number were done on vellum. The copy held by the Library of Congress is one of three known complete vellum copies. The book's three volumes are each bound in sixteenth-century white stamped pigskin bindings.

The Library of Congress obtained its copy of the Gutenberg Bible in 1930. The Bible was part of a collection of 3,000 fifteenth-century books purchased by act of Congress from Otto H. F. Vollbehr for $1.5 million. Before this copy of the Gutenberg Bible came to the Library of Congress it had been in the possession of the monks of the Benedictine Order in their monasteries at St. Blasius in the Black Forest and at St. Paul in Carinthia (Austria). Since 1930, except for periods of wartime, the Library has kept its Gutenberg Bible on permanent public display.

Peter M. Van Wingen

Adoration of the Magi. In Juan de Torquemada. *Meditationes seu Contemplationes devotissimae.* **[Mainz] 1479. Rosenwald Collection, Rare Book and Special Collections Division.**

The three magi in this illustration from a devotional book of 1479 suggest the opulence and splendor of African and Asian potentates as imagined by Europeans of the late Middle Ages.

larger states of Christendom experienced a period of dramatic and triumphant expansion. This period reached its apogee under the "Catholic Monarchs," Fernando and Isabel, Columbus's patrons. The very year that Columbus sailed, 1492, witnessed the final capitulation of the Moors of Granada to Christian power. It also saw the expulsion of the Jews from Spain, who were offered the cruel choice of a coerced baptism or a forced and penurious exile.

These events were by no means mere random historical coincidences. The expansive dynamism of Spain in the late fifteenth century attracted dreamers and schemers from all over Europe, Columbus among them. Columbus *might* have sailed from any Mediterranean port, but he in fact sailed from a port in newly "liberated" Spain. On the other hand the same "Spanish experience" that in some ways enabled the entrepreneurial optimism of the voyages of discovery had complicating and often sinister implications for the newly "discovered" lands and peoples. Spanish imperial policy remained more or less closely committed to a triumphalist and intolerant Catholicism increasingly defined, during the course of the sixteenth century, in terms of "racial purity." The attitudes that we today associate with the Spanish Inquisition were often second nature to the hidalgos like Hernando Cortés who flocked in significant numbers to make their fortunes in the New World. Strong voices would be raised in justification of the Spanish war against the native Americans of "New Spain" on the grounds that they were not Christians; and other voices, more sinister still, would excuse the oppression and exploitation of the conquered on purely racial grounds. It is important to point out that native Americans also found staunch defenders among Christian moral theologians like Francisco de Vitoria and Bartolomé de Las Casas. But when Columbus sailed, he took with him a shipload of mental attitudes which instinctively sought to assimilate the historically unprecedented experience of America to the precedent of El Cid's Spain.

The confusions and contrasts characteristic of the political situation in the Mediterranean world were even more marked in the spiritual sphere. Here the word that most nearly meets the situation is paradox. On the one hand the splendor and power of the Church, and especially of that of the Pope and of the bishops of the major Mediterranean cities, reached new heights. On the other hand scholastic theology, which in the thirteenth century helped create great cathedrals of human thought, had become the stultifying preserve of dull and leaden minds. Layfolk joined in the great debates that arose over seemingly abstruse issues such as the doctrine of the Immaculate Conception of the Blessed Virgin Mary. Religious belief and practice entered every sphere of popular life, often in highly emotional ways, in public processions, religious ceremonies, and preaching missions. The constant fear of the "Turkish menace" was only one part of a widespread doom-and-gloom philosophy characterized by social cruelty, anti-intellectualism, morbid asceticism, and private and hermetic mysticism, and often exemplified by popular religious leaders like Jerome Savonarola. At both the popular and the learned levels there was a widespread interest in apocalyptic theories, kabbalistic systems, number mysticism, and astrology.

At the same time we are right to characterize the Mediterranean world of the fifteenth century as a world of Renaissance, a rebirth of interest in and knowledge of the philosophical, literary, and scientific traditions of classical Antiquity. Indeed historians are no longer comfortable with the easy contrasts, once fashionable, between medieval and Renaissance attitudes. Such attitudes could, and did exist in one and the same person. Pico della Mirandola, the flamboyant young author of a famous defense of human dignity, died in the arms of the dour ascetic Savonarola. Among Columbus's strict contemporaries was Leonardo da Vinci, one of the greatest geniuses the world has ever known. The German artist Albrecht Dürer, who may be said to have begun his artistic career in the year of the first voyage, lived to see the first exquisite plundered artifacts brought back to Europe from the toppled temples of the Aztecs. The great scholar Desiderius Erasmus was another of the Admiral's contemporaries. Of Spanish notables of Columbus's day one may point to the less well known but still remarkable Francisco Jiménez de Cisneros, the Franciscan Archbishop of Toledo, primate of all Spain, and confessor to Isabel la Católica. In addition to all his strenuous pastoral, diplomatic, and political duties, Jiménez found the time to publish one of the greatest works of biblical scholarship of his age, the famous Complutensian Polyglot of 1502–1517, and to found the University of Alcalá de Henares. We shall see when we come to examine the mysterious character of the Ad-

Ignatius Loyola. Print by Hieronymus Wierix (Flemish), ca. 1553–1619. Prints and Photographs Division.

Ignatius Loyola was the founder of the Society of Jesus (Jesuits), a Catholic religious order particularly active in missionary work following its recognition by the Pope in 1540.

miral of the Ocean Sea, who was both something of a superstitious mystic and something of a genuine scholar, that he internalized a number of the paradoxical features of the spiritual world which had nourished him. The search for the spirit of the Mediterranean world in the age of Columbus leads one necessarily to question the frequently stated view that the Renaissance marks a sharp break with the attitudes of the Christian Middle Ages. It seems safer to say that the fifteenth century witnessed more marked or even extreme developments of contrasting tendencies already present in medieval Europe.

To some extent such developments were made possible by changes in material life and in technology. One remarkable technological innovation of almost incalculable importance was, of course, the invention of the printing press. Johannes Gutenberg discovered the principle of movable type at about the same moment in the 1440s that Portuguese navigators were exploring the Azores. He brought out the most famous book ever printed, his edition of the Bible, in 1451.

What did the printing press have to do with exploration and discovery? The answer turns out to be, "Quite a lot." First of all, the printing press significantly expanded the size of the European reading public. In order for people to read, two conditions must be met: they must know *how* to read, and they must have something *to* read. In many ways the first condition was more easily met than the second. Medieval manuscripts—and the word manuscript means "written by hand"—had to be individually and laboriously produced, frequently on expensively processed animal skin. They were costly and, very often, of a size and format anything but convenient for carrying about in a casual fashion. Medieval reading was in every sense a serious business, and it is not surprising that it was as a general rule limited to a small group of professionals. To understand the dramatic impact of the printing revolution of the fifteenth century, we may consider by way of analogy the impact of the photocopy revolution of our own time.

It was hardly more expensive to have a text set in movable type than it was to have it written out on vellum in a careful hand by a scribe. When the scribe was through, the net gain was one book, and there could be no practical guarantee of the strict accuracy of the finished copy to the exemplar. Once set in type, however, a printer's form could be printed off many times with only marginal additional costs. Furthermore the sheets could be proofread in advance by an author, editor, or any other informed person, to guarantee the accuracy and the uniformity of many finished and identical copies. Finally, where the production of manuscripts had been almost exclusively work done on the basis of individual commission, printed books were commodities for which there was a waiting retail market. Unbound sheets were relatively light and could be transported at low costs. The bookshop, entirely unknown in earlier times, was born almost in the same moment as the printing press itself.

The Mediterranean world was a world of cities—vibrant, polyglot, and often sumptuous commercial centers. When we stand today amid the palaces, religious houses, libraries, and public piazzas of a small city like Ferrara or Toledo, we experience a grandness far out of proportion to the modest populations of these places. Printers and booksellers—and they were often one and the same—immediately set up their shops in nearly all the cities of Europe. Not surprisingly the greatest center for learned printing soon became the

**Multiple Printing. Print by Philip Galle
(Netherlands), 1537–1612. Prints and
Photographs Division.**

Advances in printing technology in Europe
in the fifteenth century revolutionized the
intellectual world of the Renaissance. Illustrated here in a print by the Dutch artist
Philip Galle is the technique of multiple
printing.

Ship of Fools. In Sebastian Brant. *Das Narrenschiff.* **Basel, 1494. Rare Book and Special Collections Division.**

Sebastian Brant's *Das Narrenschiff* was a satire on human vanities, including, in the author's view, the desire for travel, exploration, and commerce. The work was a best-seller in its time.

crown jewel of Mediterranean cities—Venice.

There is abundant testimony to the role that reading and research played in the formation of Columbus's ideas. One of his sons gathered together one of the great libraries of Renaissance Spain. That fact is in and of itself suggestive, but we have the additional good fortune to have preserved in the Biblioteca Colombina many of the books from the original collection, including several that the Admiral himself had owned and left to his son Fernando at his death. Several, including the copy of the travels of Marco Polo, have marginal notes in Columbus's own hand. Columbus read both popular works, such as those of Marco Polo and Jean de Mandeville, and more severely scientific and philosophical tractates, such as those of Cardinal Pierre d'Ailly, an important humanistic theologian of the late Middle Ages whose works sought to reconcile the sciences of cosmology and astronomy with the disciplines of scriptural exegesis and speculative theology. Just as Columbus's project would have been unlikely without the printing press, the rapid advertisement of its success, which did much to stimulate the nearly frenetic competition which characterized the national policies of maritime exploration from the start, would also have been impossible. Columbus's famous Latin letter announcing the discoveries of the first voyage, a fine copy of which is included in the exhibition, dispersed the news to all parts of Europe nearly as rapidly as it could be dispersed today.

The printed word played its role, too, in the transmission of technical knowledge concerning cosmography, astronomy, and the art of navigation. The very large numbers of surviving copies of the *Arte de Navegar* of Pedro de Medina, one of the classics of its genre, clearly suggests the degree to which the events initiated by Columbus's journey had captured the attention of an ever-growing general reading public.

Not all writers, of course, took an approbative view of the excited self-advertisement of Columbus's voyage. It is probable that the first literary allusion to that voyage is a most unflattering one. An obscure humanist named Sebastian Brant published in 1494 the first edition of a book that was to prove to be among the most popular and perennial satires ever penned. It was called *Das Narrenschiff* (The Ship of Fools). It was soon published in a Latin edition, then translated into several foreign languages. Its woodcut illustrations reveal a close observation of contemporary marine architecture. That was not, however, Brant's interest. Brant took a sea voyage as a figure for the life of men and women. The ship itself then became the figurative arena for all sorts of foolish human behavior, the many ways in which human beings abandon religious rectitude and philosophical tranquility to chase after the world's false and fleeting pleasures. One such folly, apparently, was the expedition of Columbus in 1492. The basic idea behind The Ship of Fools, often called "medieval," was in fact quintessentially of the Renaissance. So was the idea of the *danse macabre,* or Dance of Death, the idea that the only worldly victor is Death himself. The Dance of Death is well known in many printed versions from the fifteenth century, but the most famous treatment of the theme, that by Hans Holbein published in 1538, included an image of Death felling the main mast of a storm-tossed ship as the agonized merchant-captain writhed in terror on the poop deck. One wonders what the Admiral of the Ocean Sea, as he lay dying in obscurity in Valladolid, would have made of such an image.

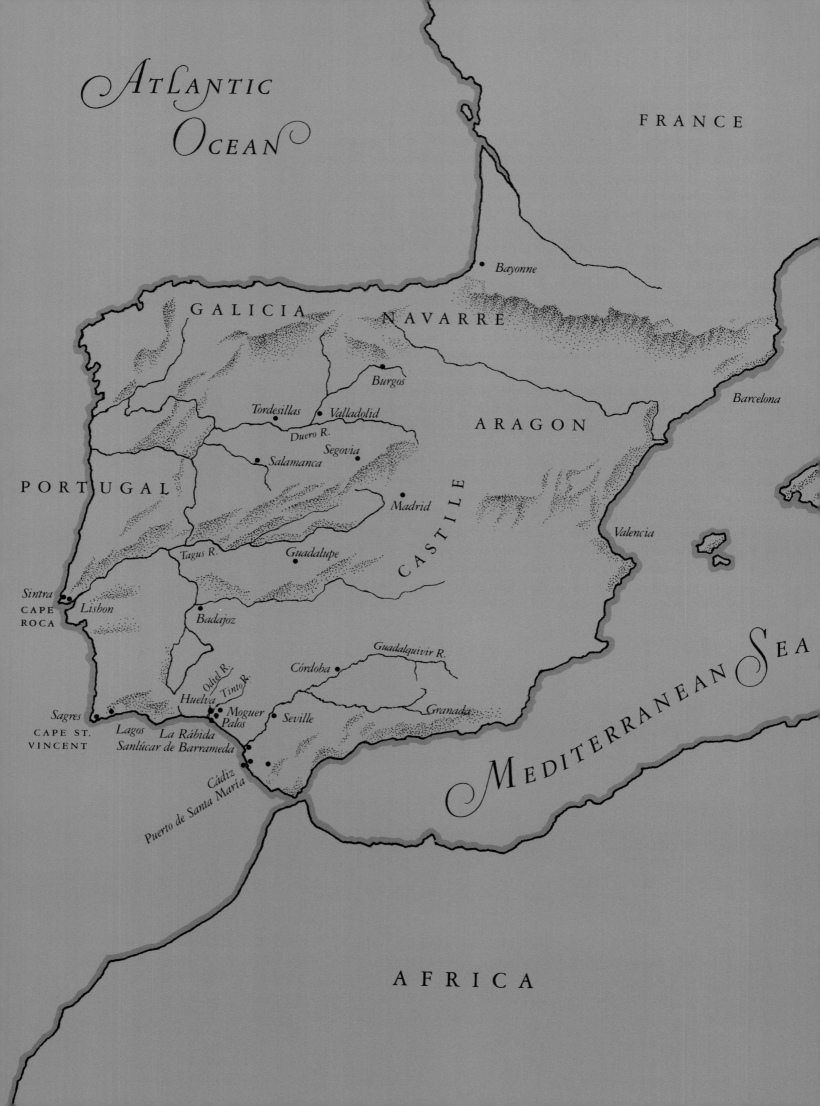

SPAIN IN THE ERA
OF EXPLORATION

by IDA ALTMAN

HE MODERN COUNTRIES of Spain and Portugal occupy the Iberian peninsula. Separated at its southern tip from North Africa by a narrow strait ten miles wide and joined to the rest of Europe only by its northern border with France, this peninsula is situated at the juncture of the Mediterranean and the Atlantic. This key geographical position played an important part in Iberia's history. From ancient times representatives of the advanced civilizations of the Mediterranean went to the peninsula, attracted by its mineral resources and rich agricultural potential. The Bible refers to trade with "Tartessos" during the time of Solomon. The seagoing Phoenicians from the eastern Mediterranean founded the colony and port of Cadiz, and the Carthaginians of North Africa succeeded them in the southern and eastern coastal areas. The Romans by far were the most thorough conquerors and colonizers of the peninsula, and their culture had the greatest and most lasting impact. By the second century A.D. most of Iberia was Romanized in language, religion, and law.

Iberia's mountainous topography also left its imprint on the history and culture of its people, partially separating it from the rest of Europe and dividing the peninsula into regions that were relatively self-contained. Sparsely populated expanses of semiarid plateau characterized much of the peninsula. But by late Roman times many areas, such as the agriculturally productive Guadalquivir Valley of the south, were fairly densely settled. The Germanic Visigoths moved across the Pyrenees into Iberia in the fifth century, eventually establishing a kingdom centered around Toledo, but they exercised relatively weak control over their Hispanic subjects. In 711 this Visigothic kingdom fell almost without resistance to invading Muslims who crossed from North Africa, apparently receiving some assistance from Christians and Jews discontented with Visigothic rule. As had been true also for the Visigoths before them, the Muslims entered the peninsula as invaders but remained as settlers. Not only were they successful colonizers but they attracted thousands of converts among the Hispanic population. Probably the majority of the people in the south converted to Islam.

The history of Iberia in the Middle Ages was dominated by the presence of the Muslims and the intermittent struggle, known as the *Reconquista* or Reconquest, of Christians to reclaim political control over the peninsula from their Muslim rivals. For much of the period up to the middle of the thirteenth century the modern countries of Spain and Portugal were divided among

Facing page: **The Iberian Peninsula in 1492. Line drawing by Stephen Kraft.**

The Iberian peninsula, which now comprises the countries Spain, Portugal, and Andorra, was, in the late fifteenth century, a collection of kingdoms and other hereditary entities with separate policies and practices.

Silk embroidered prayer shawl with a quote from the Koran. Late fifteenth century. African and Middle Eastern Division.

Panels and flags have played an important role in Islamic society as symbolic expressions of political and religious power. They were carried in processions, hung on walls, or placed on tombs. The calligraphy is a verse from the Koran (Surah 2, Verse 245) which exhorts the believers to stand firm and fight for their religious convictions as did the Children of Israel after the time of Moses.

This silk panel does not have floral and geometric decorations, as is typical of Islamic textiles, which indicates a provenance from a Mediterranean country where Islamic traditions were strong. Men were not supposed to wear silk garments, and embroidery with silk threads was strictly forbidden. The Arabs in Spain, however, were greatly interested in silk production. The geographer al-Idrisi (1109–1154) mentions 800 silk factories in Almería, many of which were still operative after the *Reconquista*.

George N. Atiyeh

Christian and Muslim states. The Muslims predominated in the south, in the region of Andalusia. The city of Córdoba, for example, was a great center of Islamic civilization, with its characteristic art and architecture, the imprint of which can still be seen today. In centers like Toledo, Muslim, Christian, and Jewish scholars collaborated in the compilation and translation of works of philosophy, science, and mathematics.

Thus Iberia's history in the Middle Ages was not exclusively one of warfare and struggle between opposing religions and cultures. There were long periods of relative harmony which fostered prosperity; significant crosscurrents of influence flowed among Christian, Muslim, and Jewish communities. Through much of this period members of one religious group could live in peace and tolerance under rulers of differing religions, and political allegiances often crosscut religious ones. The famous Christian medieval hero El Cid, for example, for a time served as ruler of the Muslim kingdom of Valencia.

In the eleventh, twelfth, and thirteenth centuries the Reconquest gathered momentum. Although it remained sporadic, both sides brought renewed zeal to the struggle, which in any case did not just concern religion but hinged as well on the quest for lands, booty, and slaves. The Christian kingdoms received some impetus and support from crusading movements underway elsewhere in Europe and the Mediterranean world. The Muslims for their part were aided by militant groups from North Africa. Christian crusading orders like the Knights of Templar at times participated directly in the Reconquest. Spaniards also formed their own similar organizations like the military orders of Santiago and Alcántara. These orders, which received grants of jurisdiction over large areas from Christian kings, would play an important role in the reconquest and resettlement of lands formerly in Muslim hands.

The cities and towns founded as Christians moved into new areas also were crucial to the consolidation of the Reconquest. These municipalities attracted potential settlers by offering tax breaks, grants of land, and other privileges of citizenship. Such incentives were necessary not only because of the sometimes risky conditions prevailing in recently reconquered areas but also because reoccupying extensive regions was a formidable proposition for the sparse populations of Christian Iberia.

Introductory page. Antiphonary [choir book]. Spain. Black, red, and blue ink on vellum. Early (?) sixteenth century. Music Division.

Antiphons are chant melodies usually sung before and after a psalm verse and are performed by the alternate singing of two singers or choirs.[1] They are used in the Divine Office as distinct from the Mass. This page contains musical notations and text from the choir part of a liturgical celebration (the feast day of St. Andrew) that was chanted by members of a religious community. As this antiphonary may have had to serve either part of or an entire choir, it was purposely made with oversized letters and notes that could be read easily from some distance. Because an emblem containing the black and white lily cross of the Dominicans is found in the border decoration along the bottom of the page, it is possible that this choir book was used by that Order.[2]

Elaborately decorated liturgical manuscripts (Bibles, Missals, Books of Hours) have a long tradition in medieval and Renaissance Europe. What is particularly striking here is the interplay between the crowded, abstract, and tightly woven interlace of the border and the space of the letters and music. The border design, with its emphasis on repetition and fluid calligraphic swirls, seems to rely on an Islamic decorative tradition rooted in the visual arts and architecture. Even here, in a religious text, there is ample evidence that despite the Arab expulsion from Spain, aspects of Islamic thought and aesthetics continued to survive and have influence. It is important to remember that the mental world of early modern Spain, although dominated by the Roman Catholic Church, included some Islamic and Jewish features as well.

Anthony Páez Mullan

Notes

1. *Encyclopedia Britannica,* 15th ed., vol. 1, "Micropaedia Ready Reference," s.v. "antiphon" and "antiphonal singing."

2. Svato Schutzner. "Ms 38" in *Medieval and Renaissance Manuscript Books in the Library of Congress: A Descriptive Catalog* (Washington: Library of Congress, 1989), vol. 1., p. 246.

Santiago de la Espada. Red and black woodcut print. In *Copilaciõ delos establecimientos dela Orden dela Cavalleria de Sātiago dela Espada*. Seville, 1503. Rare Book and Special Collections Division.

According to legend, Santiago (St. James) converted Spain to Christianity and after his death his remains were moved to Santiago de Compostela. A later addition to the legend which is associated with this illustration has Santiago riding a white steed and carrying a white banner, appearing in a radiant cloud above Christian troops battling Muslim forces. He spurs the Christians on, and many Muslim soldiers either die or flee the battlefield. This additional aspect, developed in the twelfth century, is related to both an active phase of the Christian Reconquest of the Iberian peninsula and to the founding of the Order of Santiago by Ferdinand II. The Order of Santiago was a Christian military-religious order of knights created to fight Muslims in Spain and to protect the pilgrimage route to Santiago de Compostela.[1]

The image of Santiago the Moorslayer in this detailed manual of instructions is particularly Spanish. In its emphasis on the figure of Santiago, his horse, and on the halo, crosses, swords, and banner, this image expresses both Christian invincibility and triumph. This work also clearly manifests the fusion of religious and military ideals identified with the Order.

The notion of Santiago symbolizing Christian triumph over non-Christians was part of the mental world that the conquistadores brought with them to America. To some of the Spanish, conquest and settlement of America must have seemed an extension of reconquest, only on a larger scale. Bernal Díaz and other chroniclers report that Santiago was invoked numerous times in battles against indigenous peoples. The many towns, cities, and natural features of land in the Americas that bear the saint's name are all indicative of Spanish devotion to Santiago.[2]

From the time of the Conquest, Santiago is represented in countless paintings and sculpture in America. Perhaps indigenous peoples appropriated Santiago because they were convinced of the power of this Spanish "god" who aided in their defeat. Whatever the case, the image of Santiago frequently appears in festivals, processions, and dances where, according to Johanna Hecht, he has been "transformed from terrifying divinity to benign ally."[3]

Anthony Páez Mullan

Sheep raising expanded notably in this period both because of its unique suitability to the peninsula's climate and geography and also because of the great stretches of open land that came under Christian control. The introduction of merino sheep, known for their fine wool, was a further impetus to the expansion of sheep raising. Wool became a leading export and mainstay of the Castilian economy.

In 1147 Christians recovered the Portuguese city and port of Lisbon from the Muslims. One hundred years later Seville was definitively reconquered as well. Granada was the sole remaining Islamic kingdom on the peninsula, which continued to be divided among several kingdoms: Portugal in the west, Castile in the center, Aragon in the east, and Navarre in the north. Of these Castile was by far the largest in area and population. Spain as such still did not exist; it would not become a completely unified nation until the beginning of the eighteenth century.

In the fifteenth century the Portuguese monarchy was stable and fairly strong, and it provided some of the impetus for early Portuguese expansion. But elsewhere in the peninsula monarchies were weak, as was true throughout Europe in the late Middle Ages. In the last third of the fifteenth century, however, an event occurred which would have great significance for the future. In 1469 Isabel, the leading claimant to the Castilian throne, married Fernando, heir to the crown of Aragon. In 1479 they ascended their respective thrones, creating a dual monarchy and dynastic unification of the two kingdoms which would pass on to their grandson Charles and his successors.

This marriage marked the first step in the forging of modern Spain. Although the political systems, economies, languages, and culture of the kingdoms remained separate and essentially unchanged, their unification at the level of the monarchy brought some advantages to both and enhanced the prestige and power of the crown, which from this time on can be considered a Spanish (rather than a Castilian or Aragonese) monarchy.

Notes

1. José M. Pita de Andrade. "St. James the Knight," essay translated from Spanish in *Santiago en España, Europa, y América* (Madrid: Editora Nacional, 1971), pp. 663–64.

2. Juan de Contreras. "Santiago in the Indies," essay translated from Spanish in *Santiago en España, Europa, y América* (Madrid: Editora Nacional, 1971), pp. 667–68.

3. Johanna Hecht. "Processional Figure: St. James the Moor-Killer(?)" in *Mexico: Splendors of Thirty Centuries* (New York: Metropolitan Museum of Art, 1990), p. 345.

Fortified Houses and Towers, Cáceres, Spain. Photo.

The towers and fortified houses of the southwestern city of Cáceres were the product of Iberia's long history of conquest and conflict.

[69]

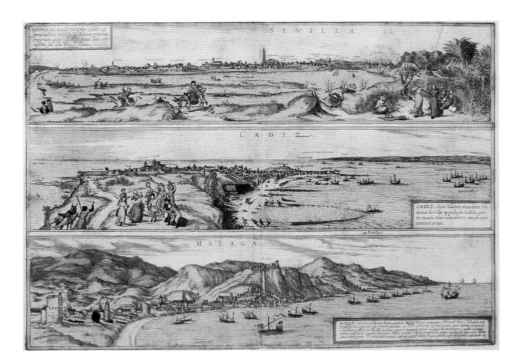

Seville, Cádiz, Málaga. In Georg Braun and Francis Hogenberg. *Civitates Orbis Terrarum,* **vol. 1. Cologne, 1612–18. Geography and Map Division.**

These three Andalusian cities were active participants in the Spanish westward expansion in the late fifteenth and the sixteenth centuries.

Fernando and Isabel—the *Reyes Católicos* as Pope Alexander VI would title them—were energetic sovereigns who undertook their policies jointly. Determined to reestablish law and order throughout their kingdoms, they traveled constantly to enforce their rule and royal will. Most of their subjects, at least in Castile, stood a good chance of having seen one or the other of their sovereigns at some time. Pious and motivated by a strong sense of duty, Queen Isabel especially was popular and highly regarded by her people.

Fernando and Isabel set out to strengthen, extend, and centralize royal power. They did not necessarily create new institutions of government to do this. They refurbished some, such as the Royal Council, and expanded others, such as the system by which representatives of the crown presided over municipal councils. They also relied more heavily than previous monarchs on the services of university-educated lawyers, who filled the ranks of the growing Spanish bureaucracy in the late fifteenth and sixteenth centuries.

The only entirely new institution introduced during their reign was the Inquisition, which became a Royal Council in 1483. The establishment of the Inquisition and expulsion of the unconverted Jews a decade later have fostered great controversy down to our times and doubtless contributed to the so-called "Black Legend" associated with Spain. Jews had lived in Spain for centuries, paying special taxes to Christian or Muslim rulers and living in their own communities. The majority pursued quite ordinary, mostly urban, occupations. A minority had acquired wealth and influence through commerce or finance and served as tax-farmers or financial advisors to kings.

Popular resentment of Jews culminated in outbreaks of violence against them throughout Spain in the late fourteenth century, and violent episodes continued during the next century. Under the circumstances many Jews converted to Christianity. As Christians they no longer were subject to the limitations which barred Jews from certain realms of public life; but as a new minority in Christian society, the *conversos* remained suspect in some eyes, especially as many maintained close ties with the Jewish community.

La Judería, Cáceres, Spain. Photo.

View from within the old walls of Cáceres of one of the city's two former "juderías" or Jewish neighborhoods. The Jewish communities in dozens of towns and cities throughout the Iberian peninsula formally ceased to exist with the Expulsion in the late fifteenth century.

Both Fernando and Isabel had Jewish and *converso* advisors in their courts on whom they relied. Most likely they hoped that the Inquisition would allow suspicion against *conversos* (who, as Christians, could be tried for heresy) to be channeled into an officially constituted tribunal sanctioned by church and crown; likewise the final decision to expel the remaining unconverted Jews probably responded to the need, as they perceived it, to control and curtail popular agitation and violence. In this sense both the Inquisition and the expulsion were popular, although both occasioned considerable protest and dissent at the time they were undertaken. In attempting to curb violence against *conversos* and Jews by taking decisive action at the highest level, the monarchs once again were acting in a manner consistent with their objectives of strengthening and centralizing royal rule.

Page from *Perush ha-Torah* by Moses ben Nahman. Lisbon, 1489 [in Hebrew]. *Hebraic Section, African and Middle Eastern Division.*

The first book printed in any language in Portugal's capital city, Lisbon, was a Hebrew book, the *Commentary on the Pentateuch* by Moses ben Nahman. It was published only three years before the expulsion of the Jews from Spain and eight years before their expulsion from Portugal.

The events of the year 1492 both symbolized and signalled the creation of the orthodox, Christian society that the Catholic kings envisioned. After a decade-long campaign the Christian forces defeated the kingdom of Granada; the last Muslim king surrendered to Fernando and Isabel in January 1492. The decree expelling the Jews from their kingdoms was signed at the end of March. Within a month they made their fateful agreement with Christopher Columbus. This act would result in wholly unforeseen opportunities for the energies and ambitions of Spain's rulers and people.

What kind of a society embarked on the enterprise to the Indies, as the lands claimed by Columbus and those who followed him came to be known in Spain? Officially the country was entirely Christian after the early sixteenth century (Portugal expelled its Jewish subjects some years after Spain did), but the pluralistic society of the Middle Ages left a legacy of diversity. *Moriscos*, descendants of Muslims, and *conversos*, descendants of Jews, formed significant minorities that were not always easily assimilated (in fact after two major rebellions in the area around Granada in the sixteenth century, the remaining *Moriscos* were expelled from Spain in the early seventeenth century). Gypsies entered the Iberian peninsula in the late fifteenth century. Although they led an itinerant existence like that of gypsies elsewhere, they did not leave the peninsula. From the middle of the fifteenth century the Portuguese brought slaves from West Africa in increasing numbers. They became a significant part of the labor force in and around Lisbon in particular and also were numerous in Seville, where they could be found working in artisans' shops and employed as domestic servants by nobles, priests, and wealthy merchants. Elsewhere in Spain well-to-do households also might boast a handful of African slaves, who functioned much as did other servants. In addition to such groups, the peninsula attracted other foreigners; thousands of people emigrated from France, settling above all in the kingdom of Aragon. And the peninsula still encompassed a striking array of closely related languages, from Catalan in the northeast and Galician in the northwest to Castilian in the center (the language that today we usually call Spanish). In the north the Basques spoke a nonromance language whose origins have never been definitely traced.

All Iberian societies were divided between nobles and commoners. By law and tradition a person belonging to the hidalgo or noble class enjoyed inherited privileges (and duties) that set that group apart from, and above, the rest of society. Among these privileges was exemption from most forms of taxation; among the duties was military service owed to the king and realm. Although doubtless the wealthiest and most powerful members of society were nobles, there were considerable variations of status and resources among the hidalgo group, which ranged from the *grandes* and *títulos* of Castile to quite humble hidalgos who might work the land or ply a trade as did their nonhidalgo peers. Many caballeros, who occupied the middle tier of the nobility, traced their origins back to the heyday of the Reconquest and the military service rendered to crown or lord by men on horseback. Probably the majority of hidalgos owed their privileged status to an ancestor who had been ennobled. Thus the nobility in general had arisen from the common estate, and both hidalgos and commoners participated in—and contributed to—a collective Iberian culture.

Commoners were the taxpayers and performed most of the productive

work of society. They could be professionals in law and medicine, clergymen, merchants, farmers, artisans, urban or rural day laborers, servants, or slaves. Commoners spanned the range from wealth to poverty, and many of them shared only their nonhidalgo status. The largest numbers of people worked in agriculture, and even individuals with skilled or specialized occupations often were part-time agriculturalists.

The class division of Iberian society was far from absolute. People of all ranks could move up and down the social and economic scale. Literacy, which could foster upward mobility, increased considerably in this period as a result of the expansion of education. Universities such as Salamanca, Alcalá de Henares, and Coimbra attracted students from the middle as well as the upper classes, and young people could study at secondary schools which were established by most municipalities in the sixteenth century.

Ties of patronage, employment, common interest, friendship, and even kinship bound members of different social and even ethnic groups to one another. Religious ideals of moral equality found expression in social organizations such as the *cofradías,* which were lay religious associations. Many of the *cofradías* welcomed members from all social and occupational groups, women as well as men. In addition to honoring a particular saint, a *cofradía*

Left: L'Espagnol. Engraving. In *Omnium fere Gentium.* Antverpiae [Antwerp], 1572. Rare Book and Special Collections Division.

This image is from a compendium of illustrations of men and women, most of them Spanish and Portuguese, in typical dress.

Right: House dress of Morisco girls. In Christoph Weiditz. *Das Trachtenbuch des Christoph Weiditz, von seinen Reisen nach Spanien.* Berlin, 1927 [facsimile of the 1529 original]. Rare Book and Special Collections Division.

Picture of Moriscos, descendants of the Muslims, from Christoph Weiditz, *Das Trachtenbuch.* . . . Weiditz's vivid depictions of the people and customs of the Iberian peninsula reflected his experience of life there.

usually performed charitable and social welfare functions for its own members and for others as well.

Iberian society was highly religious. Religious holidays filled the year. During the annual Corpus Christi festivities members of the various trade guilds would march along a route decorated with tapestries that townspeople hung from their windows. The town council would hire players to perform miracle plays (which might alternate with short comical farces) and provide bulls for the people's entertainment. Cities and towns had large religious establishments that included parish churches, monasteries, and convents. Larger cities might have cathedrals and seminaries for training the clergy. Parishes, monasteries, and even *cofradías* all maintained hospitals, although usually town councils made significant contributions to their upkeep. Religion so permeated society that the institutions (and functions) of government and church overlapped in many spheres.

Iberian society was notably urban in its orientation. Governmental, religious, and educational institutions concentrated in cities and towns, which also were focal points for local and regional economies. Weekly markets drew people and products from the villages of the surrounding countryside; annual trade fairs attracted buyers and sellers from much farther away. A noble might enjoy a sojourn in his "country house," but almost invariably his impressive urban "palace" was his principal place of residence.

The circumstances of the Reconquest had endowed cities with a great deal of independence and political power. Their charters often granted them authority over large districts that could include many smaller towns and villages as well as lands that belonged specifically to the municipality (in addition to lands set aside for the common use of the citizens). In part because of the independence and distinctive history of the towns and cities, in part because individuals tended to act collectively through associations or corporations to express their interests, people identified strongly with their particular place of origin and residence—their pueblo (a word which means both a place and the people who live there)—and its surrounding area, or *tierra*.

The men and women who went to America carried with them this allegiance to their home towns. Once there they associated with relatives and compatriots from home, wrote letters and sent back money, and often returned to visit or even to stay. If they did return permanently, they usually settled down in their home towns. Back home they often encouraged younger family members or acquaintances to go off to America, perhaps giving them some help in getting their start or referring them to relatives or friends still in the Indies.

Who decided to go to America? Almost from the very beginning people from virtually all ranks and occupations participated in the move to the Indies. The very wealthiest nobles or most destitute paupers did not go, but almost everybody else did—artisans, farmers, priests, notaries, merchants, and bureaucrats. Because of the high cost of the journey, many people traveled as the servants or employees of others, although they usually did not remain in service for long after arriving, given the kinds of opportunities that awaited. Naturally there were large numbers of young men, since people not yet established with family or occupation would be most likely to relocate. But relatively few even of the young men really went alone. They traveled with relatives or friends or as servants, or they went to join someone already

Obseruauit ac delineauit Georgius
Houfnaglius   Anno 1565.

**San Juan del Foratche, Views of Gir-
alda, Moorish Tower, and Seville. In
Georg Braun and Francis Hogenberg.
Civitates orbis terrarum. Cologne,
1612–18, vol. 5/6. Geography and Map
Division.**

The Giralda, formerly the minaret of a
Muslim mosque, became the bell tower of
Seville's cathedral.

Hispalis [Seville]. In Georg Braun and Francis Hogenberg. *Civitates orbis terrarum.* Cologne, 1612–18, vol. 5/6. Geography and Map Division.

In this plate, the Netherlandish artist, Georg Hoefnagel, portrays Seville frontally from a raised point of view. This is one of many lavish color city views in an ambitious, multivolume atlas including Europe, America, and the Near East. The work was the product of several contributors. Many of the city plans incorporate a sense of perspective reflecting the latest in Renaissance cartographic technology as well as the visual aesthetic typical of the age.

By 1580 Seville, with more than 130,000 inhabitants, was the largest city of Spain.[1] It had a long, prominent history from Roman, Islamic, and medieval times. Culturally di-

there. Over time increasing numbers of women, married couples, and family groups emigrated.

The emigrants to America carried with them their experiences and their culture—their language, religious beliefs and practices, notions of family and kinship, political institutions, loyalty to home, understanding of themselves in relation to the world—and their expectations of what they could accomplish in the Indies. Few went with the objective of learning about the new lands and peoples they would encounter. They were drawn to America by the prospect of a better life for themselves and their children, which largely meant replicating as much of the old life as possible but in much improved economic circumstances. In the Indies they had to adjust to a context quite different from that of home. Ibero-American societies began to take shape in part as a result of the adaptations that Iberian emigrants made to the new situation they found. The indigenous peoples among whom they found themselves constituted the other crucial factor in the equation that produced the postcontact societies of America.

verse, during the sixteenth century it may have counted several thousand African slaves and Moriscos in its population. However, its wealth and prestige grew rapidly toward the end of the fifteenth century due to Columbus's explorations and Spanish colonization of America. Many explorers and emigrants sailed from Sanlucar, which served as Seville's deep water port on the Guadalquivir River. As a center of agriculture and industry as well, Seville began to provide finished goods, clothing, and agricultural products not yet available in the colonies. In 1503, *la Casa de Contratación,* or the House of Trade, was founded in Seville, assuring the city's control over commerce and trade with America. Products and precious metals, especially silver, imported from the Americas, created new wealth for merchants and nobles and stimulated the financing and construction of public buildings and churches.

Seville is depicted as large (spanning the entire width of the illustration) yet orderly, remaining within the confines of the old Roman wall. Legends hanging from decorative limbs on the left and right identify some of the principal buildings, churches, bridges, and natural features associated with the city. The skyline is dominated by the clearly visible cathedral and bell tower (*la Giralda*) crowned by the figure of faith. Other notable features include the Guadalquivir River, the *Torre de Oro,* the royal palace of the Alcázar, and San Marcos (a church in *mudéjar* style noted for its high tower).

Two prominent scenes in the foreground, out of scale with the city and surrounding landscape, attest to Hoefnagel's "irrepressible passion for anecdote."[2] They depict the beating of a handcuffed cuckold and the public execution of a pimp (being stung to death by bees) and reflect the theatrical nature of public punishment for sexual crimes and other offenses that were of concern to both political and ecclesiastical authorities in this large and often unwieldy metropolis.[3]

Anthony Páez Mullan

Notes

1. Richard L. Kagan, ed. *Spanish Cities of the Golden Age: The Views of Anton van den Wyngaerde* (Berkeley: University of California Press, 1989), p. 327.

2. J. Kenning. "The 'Civitates' of Braun and Hogenburg," in *Imago Mundi* 17 (1963), pp. 41–44.

3. Mary Elizabeth Perry. *Crime and Society in Early Modern Seville* (Hanover, N.H.: University of New England Press, 1980), pp. 139–42.

CHAPTER FIVE

MAPS, NAVIGATION, AND WORLD TRAVEL

by JOHN FLEMING

AVIGATION, THE ART of transporting people and material goods over water, is as ancient and as ubiquitous as civilization itself. Nearly all peoples, with the exception of a few land-locked tribes of desert and forest dwellers, had developed more or less effective systems of water transportation by the dawn of written history. In the ancient Near East and Egypt, in ancient Greece and ancient Rome, and in the Mediterranean Christian and Islamic worlds of the Middle Ages which were their heirs, water travel, the art of navigation, was indispensable to both commercial enterprise and military empire alike.

There are essentially three ways of propelling a piece of floating wood over a watery surface, often used in combination: to make use of natural currents and flows; to apply mechanical force, pushing or pulling, to the floating object; and to use the power of the wind caught in sails. Of these the third was naturally the most effective means of maritime commerce in the premodern world.

The European world of sailing and of sailors was already very ancient in Columbus's time. The epic poems of Homer, among numerous other ancient works, give vivid evidence of the sophistication and elaboration of ancient Mediterranean merchant and military navies. There were, of course, important centers of navigation in other parts of the world, and other parts of Europe. One thinks in particular of the island and coastal peoples of the North Atlantic, and of the extraordinary maritime feats of the Vikings, or of the important military and commercial fleets of the Turks and Islamic peoples of the southern Mediterranean. Furthermore, by the late fifteenth century Spanish and, especially, Portuguese sailors had already gained substantial experience sailing the waters of much of the African coast and the Atlantic islands nearest to the European mainland. This recent experience had led to innovations, some of them of a dramatic character, in the design of ships and in the techniques of navigation. Yet maritime cultures, like other cultures, are regional. The Arawak islanders whom Columbus encountered had never before seen large sailing ships, to be sure, but the Spanish sailors would never before have seen their vast sea-going canoes. What the age of discoveries chiefly accomplished in maritime terms was to link, on a worldwide basis, previously self-contained commercial and navigational systems. The maritime world was almost by definition comparatively cosmopolitan. In a famous letter Columbus speaks of learning from peoples of all "sects"—including Eastern Chris-

Facing page: **Portolan Chart of the Mediterranean World. Mateo Prunes [Majorca] 1559. Vellum. Geography and Map Division.**

A cartographic revolution occurred in the Mediterranean world in the thirteenth century with the emergence of a new type of chart, the portolan chart. This coincided with the surge in seafaring activity and Atlantic exploration which began before the end of that century.

Portolan charts were the first true charts in which medieval speculation and fantasy gave way to scientific cartography based on experiment and observation, utilizing the mariner's compass. The charts in their earliest examples were limited to the Mediterranean and Black Seas and the Atlantic coasts of southwestern Europe. Oriented with north at the top, portolan charts depicted the coasts with a high degree of accuracy. The format and conventions established early in the development of portolan charts were closely adhered to for several centuries.

This colorful portolan chart of the Mediterranean and western Europe was drawn on vellum in 1559. The mapmaker, Mateus Prunes (1532–1594), was a leading member of a family of Majorcan cartographers who lived and worked on that island from the early sixteenth to the late seventeenth century.

Although most portolan charts were intended for use at sea, some, including this one, were prepared for wealthy merchants and royal patrons who kept them on land, where there was a better chance of survival.

It has a system of wind or compass roses centered in the Tyrrhenian Sea just east of Sardinia drawn in a typical portolan style. There are five decorative thirty-two-point compass roses, the largest of which is in the Atlantic Ocean west of the Iberian peninsula. Eight wind heads are drawn at the edges of the chart. Decorations, both symbolic and real, abound. One can find such animals as elephants and camels as well as a giraffe, unicorn, dragon, lion, and gazelle. A camel caravan is shown heading north in the vicinity of what is now Algeria. Kings and other rulers are found in rich tents emblazoned with heraldic symbols. Among them are the King of France with his fleur-de-lis and the Emperor of the Holy Roman Empire with his double eagle. In keeping with ancient cartographic custom, perhaps derived from Roman maps, there are several pictorial representations of cities and other important places, including Barcelona, Genoa, Venice, Mount Sinai, and Cairo.

The chart depicts the Mediterranean Sea, the Black Sea, part of the Red Sea, the Atlantic coast of Africa from Cape Spartel to Senegal, and the European coast to northern Scandinavia. Both real and mythical islands appear in the northwest. The real ones include Fixlanda (Iceland) and Isola Verde (probably Greenland).

Among the mythical islands are Isola de Brazil and Isola de Maydi, the latter possibly a name of Arabic origin that first appeared on the 1325 map by Angelino Dalorto.

Place names are recorded in great detail, with red ink used for major ports and coastal features. River mouths and nearby shoals and islands are shown in exaggerated and stylized form. Coastlines are shown for large islands, but smaller islands are described in various solid colors without too much care for scale or possession. Detailed information about the interior geographical features is usually omitted in portolan charts.

John A. Wolter

tians, Jews, and Muslims. When he came to set sail into uncharted waters from a port in the south of Spain, he did so as a sailor whose technology, vocabulary, and mental universe had been formatted by the international culture of uncounted generations of Mediterranean sailors before him.

Columbus, like most of his contemporaries, will strike the modern sensibility as a mixture of irresolutions if not contradictions. He had the power of keen empirical analysis needed by anyone whose very life would often depend upon the correct interpretation of meteorological signs. He was an experienced sailor, and a courageous one. Yet his thinking about the sciences of cosmography and navigation was in fundamental ways controlled by a whole range of traditional or mythic ideas—deriving from the ancient geographers, from the Bible, and from the popular religion of his day—that we should regard as anything but scientific in character.

Modern tools of navigation are so scientifically accurate and reliable that it may be difficult to imagine the difficulties sailors faced in earlier times. A fifteenth-century navigator attempting to sail a ship purposefully between two points, between Genoa and Barcelona let us say, needed to know a number of things, including the location of the fixed points, the location of his ship, the direction in which he moved, and the speed at which he moved. A sailor of Columbus's day facing such navigational challenges had certain technological aids at his command. These included calibrated measuring instruments on the one hand, and on the other more or less reliable maps and charts. Ancient sailors depended whenever possible on the direct evidence of their own eyes, trying to stay within the sight of land and of particular natural or artificial features we still call landmarks. When a navigator could see no landmarks, either because of darkness or atmospheric conditions or because the ship was beyond eye-sight distance of land, he could still make a more or less accurate estimate by observing the ship's comparative position in relation to the sun or certain stars.

From time immemorial the star of greatest navigational importance in the northern hemisphere, because of its nearly fixed position in the northern sky, was the prominent member of the constellation Ursa Minor (Little Bear, our Little Dipper). This star was also known by many other names: the Cynosure, the *bucina* (cow's horn), the North Star, the Pole Star, the *Stella maris* (Star of the Sea). By this last name it was associated with the Blessed Virgin Mary, thought of as the figurative, and in a certain sense the literal protector and guide of Christian sailors. Location, having an idea of where a ship actually is at a given moment, is no simple task.

Certain aspects of a Mediterranean maritime apprenticeship could prepare would-be world travellers only imperfectly. The Mediterranean was comparatively wide in the east-west direction but comparatively narrow in the north-south. Sailors had no real way of fixing longitude, or location on the east-west axis; but the possibilities were finite, and the seas very well known from long experience. The assessment of latitude, or location on the north-south axis, could often be rather rough-and-ready without disastrous practical results. Sailing the Ocean Sea was something else altogether. Portuguese explorers of the African coast in the 1480s, discovering that the Cynosure was no longer even visible in southern waters, developed a navigational technique of measuring solar declination.

Direction was thought of primarily in terms of *wind* direction, that is,

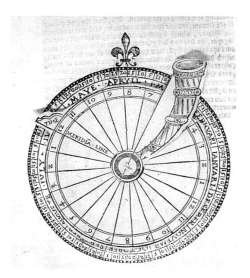

direction *from,* and what we now think of as the compass points were in origin wind directions. The names of the winds, some of which are still current in Mediterranean lands, were often evocative and romantic. The Greco, or Greek wind blew from the east; the chilly northern wind, coming from across the Alps, was Tramontana (i.e., transmountain); and so on. The four cardinal wind directions were subdivided with considerable thoroughness. A diagram reducing these subdivisions to visual form was called a wind rose. There are many beautiful examples of wind roses in maps and charts in the Library's collections.

Even when no landmarks were visible and the heavens were obscured by clouds, sailors could also estimate location and direction with the help of a compass, a device that exploits the natural attraction of a light magnetized needle for the magnetic north pole. The origins of the mariner's compass are somewhat obscure, but the instrument was known to Mediterranean sailors at least as early as the twelfth century. The needle, resting on a lightweight piece of buoyant material, was made to "float" freely in an encased liquid. When the needle became attached to a card with painted, fixed positions for north and east, the compass as we know it today came into being. By the fifteenth century a well-made compass would be expected equipment for an ocean-going ship of any size. The needle *always* pointed north, though as Christopher Columbus was in fact apparently the first to discover, it did not agree absolutely with readings taken from the North Star. There were a number of other devices which a navigator could use to take readings of latitudinal location at different times of the day or night as, in the view of sailors of those times, the heavenly bodies moved about the earth in their timeless paths. These included the astrolabe—an ancient Greek invention preserved for western Europeans, like so much else in Greek culture, by the Arabs—the cross-staff, and the quadrant. Many of these beautiful tools have survived and can be seen today in maritime museums. The sixteenth-century Caspar Vopel globe in the Library's Geography and Map Division exemplifies the exquisite workmanship typical of such instruments (see Chapter 1).

Another category of navigational aids very richly represented in the Library's collection consists of maps and charts. Old maps are of many different kinds, and many of them differ so dramatically from their modern counterparts as to be unintelligible to us without the guidance of experts. Some of

Left: **To fynde the hour with the instrument [hour guide]. In Martín Cortés. *Arte of Navigation.* London, 1589. Rare Book and Special Collections Division.**

The sixteenth-century English translation of the mariner's manual of Martín Cortés included various visual aids, including a cutout paper astrolabe, or hour gauge, with movable parts.

Center: **Ship. In *De insulis in mari Indico nuper inventis.* [Christopher Columbus] [Basel] 1494. Thacher Collection, Rare Book and Special Collections Division.**

This woodcut illustration of an "ocean ship," adorning an early edition of Columbus's epistolary announcement of his "discoveries," shows the distinctive architecture of the late-fifteenth-century caravel.

Right: **Maris Stella sucurre nobis [illustration of a compass with the Virgin and Child in the center]. In Rodrigo Zamorano. *Compendio del arte de navegar.* Seville, 1588. Rare Book and Special Collections Division.**

The North Star (also known as the lodestar, Cynosure, and the *stella maris* or Star of the Sea among many other names) played a central role in early astral navigation in the Northern Hemisphere. Columbus and other Mediterranean world sailors associated this star with the Virgin Mary, one of whose titles was Star of the Sea.

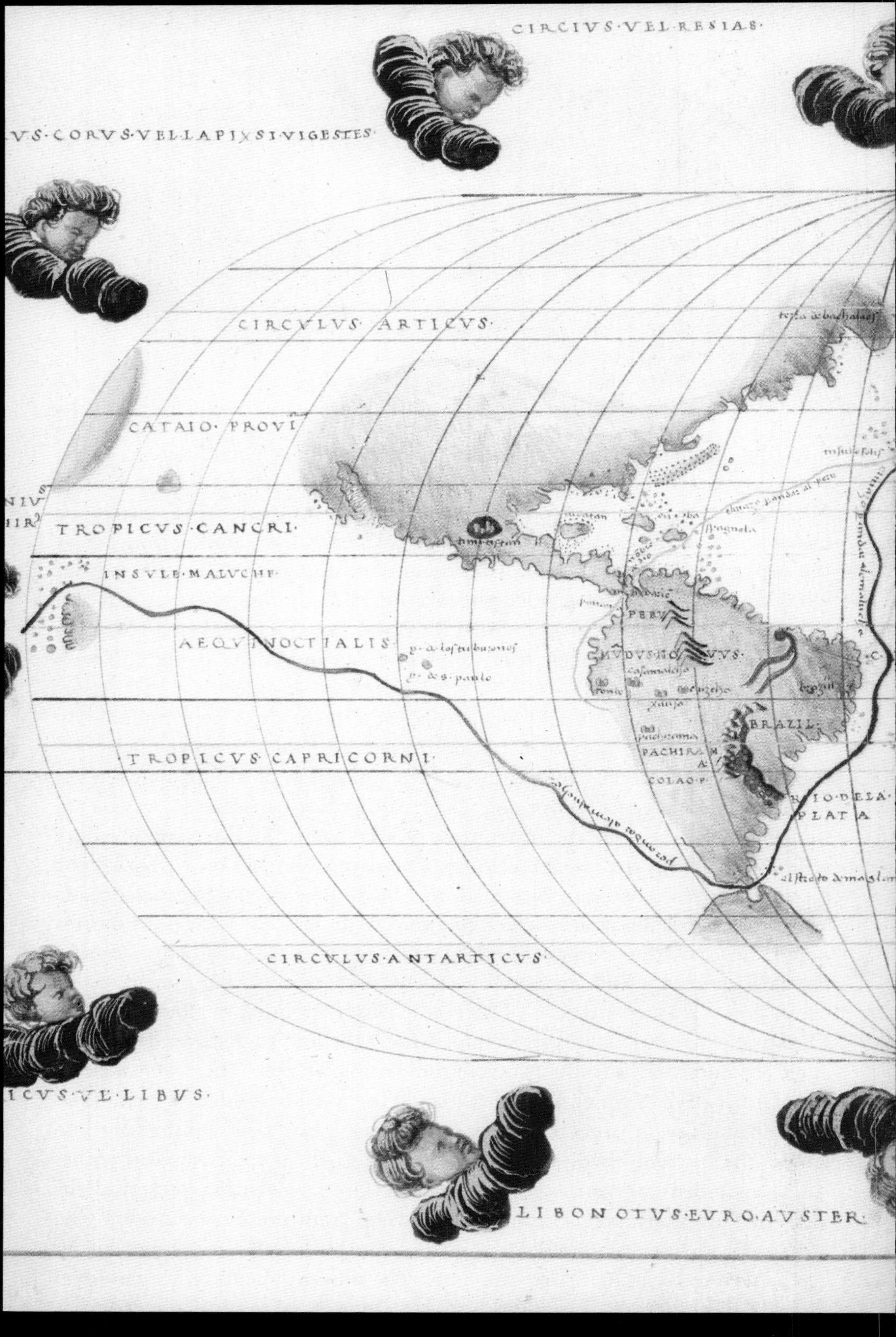
CIRCIVS·VEL·RESIAS·
VS·CORVS·VEL·LAPIXSI·VIGESTES·
CIRCVLVS·ARTICVS·
CATAIO·PROVI
TROPICVS·CANCRI·
INSVLE·MALVCHE
AEQVINOCTIALIS
PERV
MVDVS·NOVVS
BRAZIL
TROPICVS·CAPRICORNI·
PACHIRA
RIO·DE·LA·PLATA
CIRCVLVS·ANTARTICVS·
ICVS·VL·LIBVS·
LIBONOTVS·EVRO·AVSTER·

World Map with Route of Magellan. In Battista Agnese. [*Portolan Atlas*] Venice, ca. 1544. Vellum Chart Collection, Geography and Map Division. (See also pages 2 and 54.)

This rendering of knowledge of the world, with Magellan's route of circumnavigation included, reflected the extent of new found information that Mediterranean explorers obtained within fifty years of Columbus's 1492 arrival in America. The former Europocentric world view had fallen prey to new ideas and new places.

¶ E homincia dalla perfia la fuo prima
enfino aquel gran fiume fuol ourare
indo chiamato z enne fatto iftima
perche molrabondate quefta pare.

e nel numero fono oelle chiamate
e yna bumana e non piu nature
fiche perfectamente giudichate
cofi moftral potere idio oiuino
ficome tratta el ooctoz aguftino

Title page with fantastic figures. In Giu-
liano Dati. *Il Secondo Cantare dell'India.*
Rome, 1494/95. Rosenwald Collection,
Rare Book and Special Collections Division.

Among the early poetic reactions in Europe
to the news of Columbus's journey were the
"Songs of the Indies" by the Italian Giuli-
ano Dati. The work celebrated, in word
and picture, many of the imaginary marvels
that Europeans thought were found in
Asia.

the several rich cartographic traditions that flourished in pre-Columbian
America, for example, are not yet understood by scholars, and the same may
to a certain extent be said of early European maps themselves. Such maps
shared few of our modern cartographic conventions, for their purpose was not
to convey accurate information about distances and geographical direction
but to state symbolic truths, largely of a religious nature, about a certain
conception of the ordering of the world. For example, the most common
cartographic genre in ancient Europe, the so-called T-O map, was of this
kind. This map of the world essentially looks like a majuscule Roman "T"
framed within a majuscule "O." The half circle and two-quarter circles defined by this arrangement were the three known continents, each believed to
have been peopled by the descendants of one of the three sons of the biblical
Noah (see Genesis 5.32). In this schematic map vast Asia is at the top, Europe on the lower left, and Africa on the lower right. The letters themselves
represented the idea of the earth (*Terra* in Latin) encircled by the immeasur-
able Ocean Sea (*Occeanus*). In another "reading" the vertical bar of the "T"
represented the Mediterranean, the horizontal crossbar the line defined by an
imaginary union of the Don and Nile Rivers. The "T" was also a so-called
"tau cross," an emblem of ancient mystical significance in the Christian
world, and the point of junction of the vertical and horizontal elements was
taken to be Jerusalem, imagined as the center of the world.

Modern cartographic convention imagines north at the "top," but in the
ancient system the literally superior direction was east, the direction of Jeru-

salem as viewed from European perspective. We still speak of grasping the fundamental realities of a situation as "orientation." T-O maps could be more or less elaborate, but they always conveyed a rather simple symbolic idea. Indeed it is probably better to think of them as pictorial emblems or symbols standing for the idea of the world than as maps in any modern sense. When, in their attempts to communicate with native populations whose languages they had as yet not completely mastered, the first Franciscan missionaries in Mexico devised a picture language, they simply assumed that this emblem of the T-O would be universally understood to mean "world."

The much more elaborate *mappae mundi* or world maps, of which several spectacular examples have survived from medieval times, combined the religious symbolism of the T-O maps with elaborate scenes from imaginary travel posters: "portraits" of the legendary Prester John, illustrations of pygmies fighting with cranes, or of fully armed Amazons, or of dog-headed people joined in solemn conclave. Unlike the T-Os, the *mappae mundi* were often huge in size and opulent in their artistry. Though almost entirely lacking in any practical geographical information, replete instead with fabulous lore of every conceivable sort, many of the *mappae mundi* were very learned. The famous Catalan Atlas of 1375, which exists in a unique copy in Paris and is represented in our exhibition by a sumptuous facsimile, combines beautiful pictorial art with what is in effect a vernacular encyclopedia of medieval scientific, ethnographic, and technological lore.

No one ever used a T-O map for practical guidance in planning a trip, nor can we imagine a sea captain consulting something like the great world map in Hereford Cathedral in order to plan a course for his ship. Even those maps that were actually put to practical use by early seafarers and that most nearly conform to modern cartographic expectations—the "Ptolemies" and the portolan charts—depict a practically imaginary world. Ptolemy, an enormously influential geographer and astronomer of the second century, was the classical authority both for the geocentric conception of our planetary system which was only definitively challenged by Copernicus and his followers, and for the system of the grid of longitude and latitude used to describe the earth's sphere. The universal acceptance of Ptolemy's general scheme of things makes it impossible to believe the popular modern fiction that Columbus or any other competent cosmographer of his time could have thought that "the earth was flat" or that there was a danger of "falling off the earth." In the Renaissance, printed editions of Ptolemy's geography were numerous, and the Library's collection of them is among the richest in the world. Compared with the symbolic *mappae mundi,* Ptolemy's map has a certain initial reassuring familiarity about it. Only on closer examination do the alarming aberrations become obvious. The continents of North and South America, naturally, did not exist in Ptolemy's world, or on his map. The successful Portuguese expedition around the tip of Africa and across the Indian Ocean to the Asian subcontinent exposed another prominent inaccuracy of his geographical conceptions. The famous Toscanelli map which may have played an important role in Columbus's thinking was essentially a variant visual interpretation of Ptolemy's geographical speculations. Ptolemy's useful conventions of longitude and latitude have proved of permanent value, but his errors, like those of so many others, also played their part in the history of Columbus's expedition, since by Ptolemaic reckoning the distance travelled to the unknown

Map of the World. In [Donnus Nicolaus Germanus] *Cosmographia, Claudius Ptolemaeus.* **Ulm, 1482.**

What maps and geographical works influenced educated Europeans in the final quarter of the fifteenth century is a question that crosses the mind of many persons studying the Age of Discovery. Numerous contemporary items may be suggested. Certainly a principal work was Claudius Ptolemy's *Geography* or *Cosmography,* the most popular geographical work to be printed from movable type in the fifteenth century. Originally compiled by the Alexandrian geographer, astronomer, and mathematician Claudius Ptolemy in the second century A.D., it was translated from Greek into Latin in Florence, Italy, about 1410. Numerous hand copies were made of the text and accompanying maps. The rising popularity of the *Geography* among Western European scholars and the nobility made it a perfect candidate for duplication on the recently developed printing press.

The map of the world here reproduced, beautifully illuminated with twelve wind heads, is one of thirty-two maps illustrating the edition of the *Cosmographia* issued from the press of Lienhart Holle of Ulm, Germany, on July 16, 1482. Holle's edition was the first to be printed north of the Alps and the first to include maps printed from woodcuts. The world map was printed from a woodcut executed by Johannes of Armsheim, whose name appears in the upper border. To produce his printed edition, Holle used a manuscript copy prepared under the direction of the Benedictine Monk known as Donnus Nicolaus Germanus. Today, the original codex is preserved in Wolfegg Castle, Württemberg, Germany.

The map of the world reflects the Ptolemaic world view. The old or known inhabited world (*oikoumene*) is depicted as extending 180 degrees east and west, but in reality it covers only 105 degrees of longitude. This elongation, greatly shortening the unknown portion of the earth, was to influence navigators such as Christopher Columbus for many years. Also depicted is

Ptolemy's mistaken notion that the Indian Ocean was an enclosed body of water, an idea that was to be disproved only five years later by the successful rounding of the Cape of Good Hope by Bartholomeu Dias of Portugal.

New information began to find its way into the classical representations then in circulation in Western Europe, and the 1482 world map was no exception. Nicolaus Germanus, for example, extended the map northward to show Iceland (correctly positioned north of the British Isles) and Greenland (incorrectly shown as a peninsula of Europe). Raleigh Skelton in the introduction to the facsimile edition of *Claudius Ptolemaevs Cosmographia, Ulm, 1482* (Amsterdam, 1963) noted that this is "the earliest printed delineation of Greenland, Iceland and the North Atlantic [on a world map]; and this was to exercise a potent influence in the cartography of the early 16th century."

Richard W. Stephenson

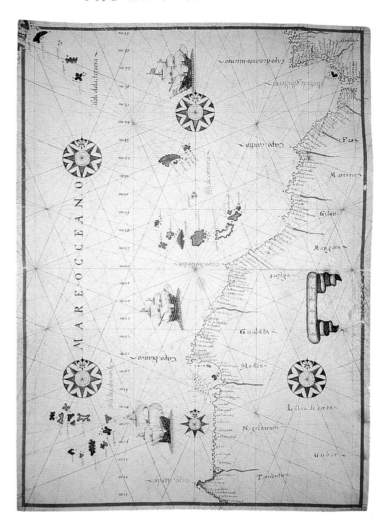

Portolan Chart of Northwest Africa, Azores, Madeira. [Portolan Atlas] [Jaume Oliva] [ca. 1560]. Vellum Chart Collection, Geography and Map Division.

Portuguese exploration in West Africa and in the islands off the African coast from the middle of the fifteenth century contributed mightily to travels,such as those of Columbus. This portolan chart records a comparatively sophisticated and detailed knowledge of the northwest African coast.

lands of the American islands *should* have taken him to Asia. By the early sixteenth century Martin Waldseemüller was publishing world maps including the Americas, in part with fair accuracy, and by 1578 Gerardus Mercator, who had revolutionized European cartography with his "projection" in 1569, could publish an edition of Ptolemy as an antiquarian enterprise.

The maps most prized by Mediterranean sailors for their practical usefulness were the portolan charts, a term of somewhat uncertain origins. These charts, often drawn on vellum with great skill and accuracy, were the "road maps" of the sea. They recorded the names of seaports, coastal towns, and prominent landmarks around the Mediterranean littoral. They often also suggested possible routes, prevailing winds, and other useful practical information. The Library's impressive collection of portolans clearly traces the way in which this kind of map developed by Mediterranean traders naturally became the model for the Portuguese explorers of the African coast and, later, for the Spaniards in America. The European explorations, of course, greatly stimulated the need for new maps and new techniques of mapmaking, so that the sixteenth century is naturally one of the most productive periods in cartographic history. The period saw the development of the modern atlas, or portfolio of maps, to be used both for the practical purposes of sailors and to stimulate and satisfy the burgeoning geographical curiosity of a European reading public that wanted to keep up with the latest discoveries. There were many books of popular geography published during this period, including a

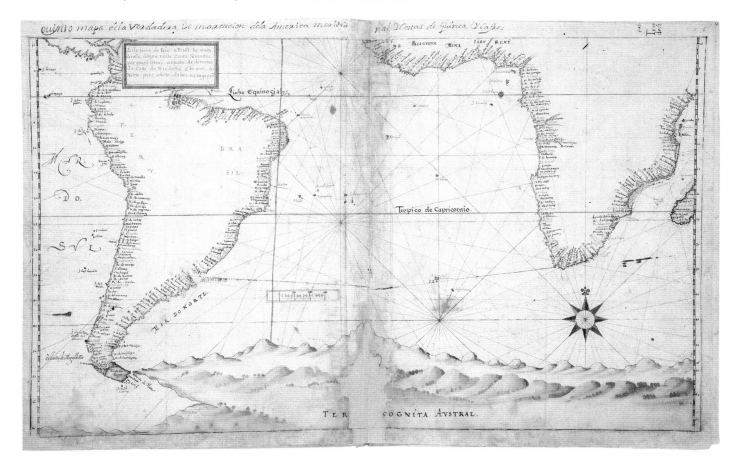

series of *isolarios,* collections of maps and descriptions of the islands of the world partly stimulated by the Iberian discoveries off the African coast, one of the earliest of which was that of Bartolomeo da Sonetti (1485).

There was by Columbus's time a fairly extensive library of scientific or pseudoscientific literature dealing with geography, with more or less technical aspects of astronomy, cosmology, and navigation, and with the real or pretended observations of travellers. The Library's collection of such books is particularly rich, and they form an important part of the exhibition. What strikes the modern reader in many of these books is their extraordinary melange of sound observation and fantastic fib. The genre of descriptive geography, in particular, authorized the search for "wonders" and "marvels." The classical geographers, such as Pliny, Ptolemy, Strabo, and Solinus, continued to be widely read, their ancient errors and inventions of monstrous races and exotic opulence regarded as absolutely authoritative. Among several medieval astronomers whose work remained to some degree influential was the Englishman John of Hollywood, usually called by his Latin name, Johannes de Sacrobosco, whose treatise entitled *The Sphere* taught generations of young students the spherical conception of the earth.

Before the age of exploration European experience of "the East"—an elastic term that could mean any part of the vast territory between Damascus and Tokyo—was, of course, extremely limited, and European conceptions of the exotic Orient were largely literary in character. That conception began with the vision of the earthly paradise that, according to the Bible, God had created "eastward in Eden." Many early travellers sought this lush, verdant,

Atlantic side of South America with the Line of Demarcation. In João Teixeira. *Taboas geraes de toda a navegacão divididas e emendadas por Dom Ieronimo de Attayde.* **Manuscript atlas. 1630. Geography and Map Division.**

From the fifteenth through the seventeenth centuries, the Spanish and Portuguese crowns vied for possessions across the globe. In 1493, Pope Alexander VI issued a papal bull creating a longitudinal line of demarcation which divided the world between Spain and Portugal and effectively gave Spain most of America. The two countries held several diplomatic congresses to dispute the placement of the line of demarcation and to determine thereby how much of Brazil the Portuguese could claim. The above map shows the "true demarcation of southern America," according to the title later added in Spanish by Francisco de Seixas y Lovera (1650–1705/6). In a letter to Charles II (1661–1700), Seixas states that he acquired the Teixeira atlas from the Portuguese Royal Library and Archives "using intelligence and money." He later presented the atlas to the king so that "His Majesty use it in the Congresses against Portugal."

The works of João Teixeira closely follow Portuguese undertakings in the sixteenth and first half of the seventeenth centuries. Little is known about Teixeira, except what can be deduced from his works. He was appointed cartographer of the *Armazéns da Casa de Guiné e India* in 1602. Since the Spanish and Portuguese crowns were officially united in 1580, Teixeira's maps were known to various Spanish explorers. Teixeira served as Cosmographer-major briefly in his career, only signing as such in his atlases of 1648. No work of his is recorded after 1649.

This navigational chart, the fifth map in the atlas, includes rhumb lines and wind roses and lists islands, capes, rivers, and cities along the coasts of Africa and South America as they appeared in the early seventeenth century. In the inset the cartographer notes, "This land of Peru and Brazil is wider than shown in this chart which is only concerned with the routes along the coast of the South Sea [Pacific Ocean] and of the North Sea [Atlantic Ocean] for the purpose of good navigation." The southern border of the map shows an "unknown southern land" (Antarctica) covered with green hills and trees.

Interesting charts included in this unique 1630 atlas depict port cities throughout the world. One delineates Brazil and the mouth of the Amazon River. Another labels rivers and tribes in the interior of Guinea between the Senegal and Sierra Leone. A third illustrates "Mountains of Gold," "Land of Good People," "Land of Hunger," and "Barren Land," in the interior of South Africa and, along the coast, shipwrecks containing "medallions of gold." The atlas contains a world map on which the line of demarcation is drawn farther west than shown in this map, casting doubt on the accuracy of either one.

Robert L. Roy

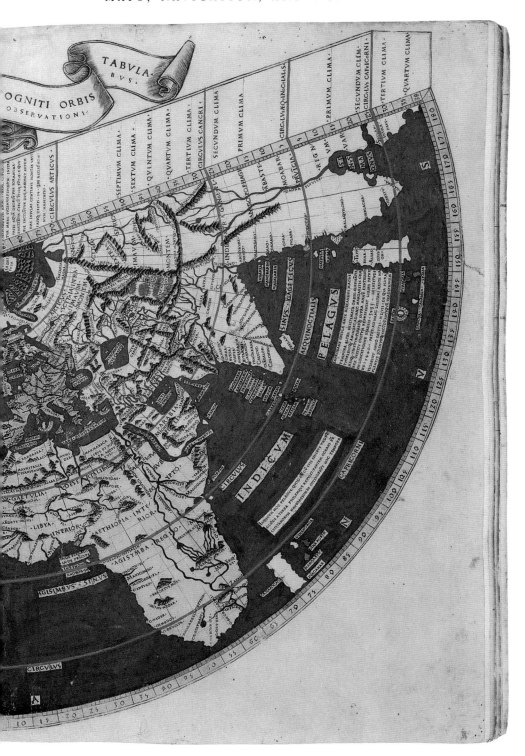

Vniversalior Cogniti Orbis Tabvla [World Map] by Joannes Ruysch. In [Cl. Ptholemaei]. *Geographia*. Rome, 1507. Geography and Map Division.

Columbus dramatically changed the world map with his first voyage to America. In the decades that followed, the classical world view of Ptolemy, encompassing an insular Eurasian continent, was replaced by a series of expanding world images derived from varying combinations of the Ptolemaic model, medieval geographical lore, and Spanish, Portuguese, and English maritime discoveries. These new concepts were best expressed graphically in the form of maps; today they provide a unique visual record of Renaissance discovery and exploration.

In 1506–1507, three printed world maps appeared for the first time that incorporated the Columbian discoveries, revolutionizing cartography: Giovanni Contarini's untitled fan-shaped or conical projection engraved by Francisco Roselli in Florence; Martin Waldseemüller's great wall map, famous for introducing the name "America"; and Johann Ruysch's *Vniversalior Cogniti Orbis Tabvla Ex Recentibvs Confecta Observationibvs*. It was particularly fortunate that the "Age of European Discovery" coincided with the invention of printing, which not only made maps cheaper and available to a wider audience but made them more likely to survive. Of these three maps, however, only the Ruysch map, reproduced here, is available today in more than one copy.

Widely circulated and influential, Ruysch's world map was engraved in 1507, one of seven new maps prepared for a reprinting of the 1490 Rome edition of Ptolemy's *Geographia*. Designed to accompany a description of the New World by Marcus Beneventanus, an Italian monk, it became available too late in the year to be included in most of the 1507 Ptolemy atlases. It is therefore generally associated with the 1508 edition. Little is known of its author, a native of Antwerp who lived in Germany. In his commentary, Beneventanus describes Ruysch as the "most learned of geographers and well skilled in depicting the globe." Scholars believe that Ruysch accompanied Bristol seamen on a voyage to the great fishing banks off Newfoundland in about 1500.

Several contemporary geographical concepts of the New World are expressed by Ruysch. In the north, Greenland and Newfoundland (reached by John Cabot in 1497) are delineated as forming a continuous coastline which merges with Asia, reflecting the belief that Portuguese and English seafarers reached this part of the Asian continent.

Cartographers of the period also were confused about the findings associated with Columbus's voyages to the West Indies, illustrated by Ruysch's attempt to depict the geography of the Caribbean Sea. The large triangular-shaped island, depicted north of the South American continent, has been identified at various times as Cuba; the east coast of Asia, mirroring Columbus's conviction that Cuba was part of the mainland; Florida; or the Yucatan Peninsula. Its western boundary is marked by a scroll, an emblematic device on maps of exploration suggestive of the unknown, which notes that Spanish ships had reached this point. In another note, Ruysch associates the island of Spagnola (Haiti/Dominican Republic) with the island of Cipango (Japan), first described by Marco Polo.

The concept of a new world finds its fullest expression in the delineation of South America, depicted as a distinct continental landmass. Designated as the "Land of the Holy Cross or the New World," the coastal details are derived from the latest Portuguese explorations and the voyages and writings of Americus Vespucius. In an inscription across the continent, Ruysch describes the region and its inhabitants. The unexplored western boundary is symbolized by a scroll announcing that "this map is left incomplete for the present, since we do not know in which direction it trends."

Ralph E. Ehrenberg

fruitful garden, and several claimed to have found it. The earliest European "travel guides," which date from the first centuries of the Christian era and which were written by or for pilgrims intent on visiting the sites made famous in Old Testament story or associated with the New Testament accounts of the life of Jesus Christ, often contained fanciful, indeed fantastic visions of "eastern" geography and peoples. The affront experienced by western Christians at Islamic control of the Holy Land was a major cause of the Crusades, which were in effect armed pilgrimages. Among other and less happy results, the Crusades of the eleventh and twelfth centuries unquestionably expanded the geographical horizons of hundreds of thousands of Europeans. Furthermore, the general failure in the Crusades excited Europe's interest in the exotic East in other ways. Europeans knew that beyond the lands controlled by their Muslim adversaries were the territories of another powerful people, the Mongols. Furthermore it had long been believed in Christian legend that the apostle Thomas had carried Christianity to India, and that somewhere in the East his successor, the priest-king Prester John, ruled over an opulent empire. In the thirteenth century the pope commissioned friar-missionaries of the new Franciscan Order to set off to find the great Khan or king of the Mongols in the hopes of converting him to Christianity and contracting him in alliance, along with Prester John if possible, in common cause against the Saracens.

As fantastic as this plan may sound, friars did undertake such a journey, and one of them, Giovanni di Pian di Carpini, wrote an extraordinary book, *The History of the Mongols,* which recounts his adventures. The books of two other world travellers, Marco Polo and Jean de Mandeville, were carefully studied by Christopher Columbus. Marco Polo, a cadet member of a prominent Venetian commercial family in the second half of the thirteenth century, travelled extensively through the Mongol Empire, had direct contact with Kublai Khan, and visited Persia, India, and China among other oriental places. It is almost by chance that he came to leave a written account of his extraordinary journey; and though his book includes a number of fabulous elements de rigueur for the genre, the main outlines of his story have the ring of truth and are confirmed by a wealth of fascinating and often closely observed detail.

Jean de Mandeville was a traveller of a different stripe altogether. In fact, it is not certain whether Jean de Mandeville ever actually existed; but there is no doubt whatsoever that the travel book published under his name was among the most successful collections of cock-and-bull stories ever written. Jean pretends to be a pilgrim-knight whose pilgrimage to the Holy Land, already sufficiently marvellous, was extended to include a comprehensive tour of the extreme Orient, including China, Japan, Malaysia, Ceylon, and a number of other island kingdoms that cannot be identified with even an approximate certainty. When Columbus arrived in the Antilles basin and began searching for or reporting the existence of cannibals, dog-headed men, and one-eyed races, he had been primed to do so by Jean de Mandeville. In fact his own most famous piece of writing, the *Journal* or daily log of the voyage of 1492, clearly reveals that he realized that one of the obligations of the "travel writer" is to surprise and delight his readers with the "marvellous," one of his favorite adjectives. One must admit that the word is apt both for the world from which he came and the world to which he sailed.

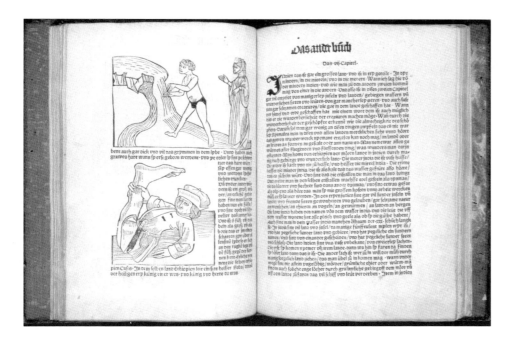

Two Figures by a Spring and a Sciapod. Woodcut print. In Jean de Mandeville. *Itinerarium*. Strassburg, 1484. Rosenwald Collection, Rare Book and Special Collections Division.

Little is known about Jean de Mandeville, the author of an eminently readable and vivid collection of travel stories based on various ancient, medieval, and contemporary sources including his own purported journeys. He was an English knight who crossed over to the European continent in 1322. His alleged years of travel in the Holy Land, North Africa, India, and the Far East are the basis of his book, *Travels,* which first appeared in French sometime between 1350 and 1375.[1] Some two hundred and fifty extant manuscript copies of the book and a considerable number of printed editions and translations all attest to the popularity of Mandeville's *Travels* in the fifteenth and sixteenth centuries.

Although Mandeville may have visited the Holy Land and the Near East, it is less likely that he journeyed to India and beyond. Consequently the reputation of his work has varied from that of an accurate account of an eyewitness observer to that of a fantastic story by a fabulous, imaginative liar.

As a popularizer and creator of a romance of travel, Mandeville influenced contemporary and later authors including Chaucer, Jean d'Arras, Christine de Pisan, and Cervantes, among others. However, beyond the incredible tales of strange people, miraculous waters, enchanted gardens and the like, Mandeville's *Travels* also embodied "the real advances in geographical knowledge and geographical thought that were made in the thirteenth century."[2] Mandeville showed that men could "sail around the world and return home safely."[3] Thus the book served as an important step in the process of what has been described as "imaginative preparation" required for actual exploration. As such, Mandeville's work was a factor in sparking the imagination and fostering a yearning for travel in would be explorers and discoverers. It was no accident that *Travels* enjoyed a second wave of popularity in the last twenty years of the fifteenth century, or that both Marco Polo and Mandeville were sources of inspiration for Christopher Columbus's voyage, as Ferdinand Columbus claimed.

Both woodcut illustrations from this German translation refer to the people of Ethiopia and seem to be particularly fanciful. The one on top shows a man and a woman standing by a spring or well, the water of which "on the day is so colde that no man may drinke thereof, and on night is so hote that no man may suffer to put his hand in it."[4] In the illustration beneath, the reader is presented with a specimen of the single-footed monster race, the sciapods. We are told that members of this race use their single foot lying on their back as a kind of parasol or shield for protection against the sun.[5]

Anthony Páez Mullan

Notes

1. Josephine Waters Bennett. *The Rediscovery of Sir John Mandeville* (New York: The Modern Language Association of America, 1954), p. 1.

2. Ibid., p. 231. Bennett reports that E. G. R. Taylor made this observation in *Tudor Geography*.

3. Ibid., p. 232.

4. Sir John Mandeville. *The Voiage and Travaile of Syr Iohn Maundeville* (London: Oxford University Press, 1932), p. 154.

5. Malcolm Henry Ikin Letts. *Sir John Mandeville: The Man and His Book* (London: The Batchworth Press, 1949) (rpt. 1971, Scholarly Press Inc.), p. 55.

Egide Charles Gustave Wappers

Anthony More

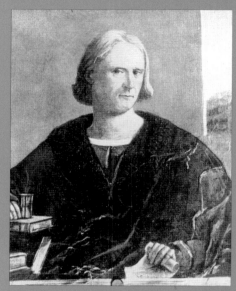

Lorenzo Lotto

Theodor de Bry

**Giuseppe Banchero (copy of
Antonio del Rincón)**

Leopold Flameng

CHAPTER SIX

CHRISTOPHER COLUMBUS
THE MAN AND THE MYTH

by JOHN FLEMING

T IS NECESSARILY misleading to commemorate Columbus's voyage of 1492 as a single "event," for the processes of cultural encounter between Europeans and Americans which it initiated were complex, varied, and in a certain sense perennial. Nonetheless when most people think of the Columbian Quincentenary they think of a single historical man, Christopher Columbus, and a single historical event over which he presided. Who was this man? For much of the 500 years that separate us from his historic voyage scholars have been asking that question. Surprisingly, perhaps, the question has received no definitive answer.

In one sense there are many Columbuses. Like Julius Caesar, Shakespeare, Napoleon, and others whose lives and works have throughout history intrigued small armies of admirers or detractors, Columbus has been remade in the image of every age and of every group of his investigators. There are dozens of published lives of Columbus, beginning with that written by his own son Fernando shortly after his death, and continuing down to this very year. Yet his life has often been less of a beacon illuminating the pages of history than it has been a mirror in which many generations have seemed to see reflected their own aspirations or anxieties. When we try to separate Columbus the man from Columbus the myth, we find surprising mysteries, contradictions, or uncertainties concerning the most basic facts of biography. There is no absolute agreement, for example, concerning the man's place of birth, his native language, his religious commitments, or the resting place of his mortal remains. We do not know what Columbus looked like, the only contemporary physical descriptions of him being so general and so stylized as to be virtually meaningless. There is a fairly large number of early portraits of the man, but it seems likely that such similarities as they share result from copying one from another rather than from any common response to an actual life model. When we turn to more subjective matters such as an assessment of his motives or an evaluation of his capacities as a fund-raiser, a sailor, a businessman, a geographer, or an administrator, the picture is even more opaque. In the pages that follow we shall review a number of the most salient facts we can say with some certainty that we know about Columbus, offer some reasonable speculations concerning his mind and character based on a reading of surviving documents, and note in passing some of the versions of Columbus that history has constructed in different times and places.

Facing page: **Six Images of Columbus.**

There is no likeness of Christopher Columbus whose claim is indisputable. The only portraits of the explorer that are from contemporaries are narrative texts by a handful of close compatriots: his son Fernando, Oviedo, and Gomera. From these we learn that his face was long, his cheekbones rather high, his nose aquiline, his eyes light grey (or blue), his complexion ruddy with freckles. His hair was reddish before it changed to white after he reached thirty. Historians who had access to Columbus's acquaintances or to primary documents, such as Herrera, Girolamo Benzoni, and Angelo Trevisan, also followed with similar descriptions.

The similarities within the written records often clash with the artistic interpretations of the Admiral. Many painters let their imagination run wild when it came to Columbus. Artists were also constrained by the artistic criteria of their period, embellishing their work within the approved canons of their own time and country. For example, in Spain during the reign of Fernando and Isabel the Catholics, portraits of individuals were usually clean shaven. The beard appeared more frequently in paintings in the Peninsula with Charles V. We note also that the ruff appeared in vogue in Spain at the end of the sixteenth century.

Two paintings are faithful to the early sixteenth-century Spanish canon of clean-shaven, with long straight hair: Lorenzo Lotto's and Antonio del Rincón's. This latter is regarded as the founder of the Spanish School and was the first painter of the Catholic monarchs. So few extant paintings are definitely attributed to him that some critics have even questioned if he was a painter. Here we show Giuseppe Banchero's copy of Antonio del Rincón's sixteenth-century painting of Columbus. This style parallels that of the portrait by Rincón's Venetian contemporary Lorenzo Lotto, who was never in Spain. Lotto's portrait was brought in 1893 to Chicago for the Columbian Exposition. The Belgian baron, Egide Charles Gustave Wappers was known both for his political and extravagant style. De Bry's engraving has been likened to a Swiss or Flemish face, but is one of the older and better known representations. The Englishman Anthony More's attempt is more akin to what we would expect with a portrait of Elizabethan England than of Spain. Leopold Flameng's rendering is more of a nineteenth-century musketeer than a fifteenth-century sailor. But all underscore the abiding influence of Christopher Columbus, known also as Cristoforo Colombo and Cristóbal Colón, on European imagination throughout history.

Everette E. Larson

De insulis in mari Indico nuper inventis [printed letter] [Christopher Columbus] [Basel] 1494. Thacher Collection, Rare Book and Special Collections Division.

In his pursuit of recognition and fame, Christopher Columbus had published in Latin a letter to the world at large concerning his "recently found islands." The 1494 Basel edition contained curious illustrations depicting the peoples and places he had encountered on his first voyage; none of the illustrations was taken from real life situations, but from the imagination of the publisher.

Christopher Columbus was born in the middle of the fifteenth century, possibly in 1451. Although the matter has been hotly debated, most scholars believe that he was born in Genoa, an important commercial and maritime center on the northwestern coast of what is today Italy, and the original form of his surname, from which the more familiar Latin form Columbus was derived, was Colombo. When he established himself in Spain, he adopted the surname Colón. His family was probably of the artisan class. According to his own testimony he went to sea at the age of fourteen, but we lack concrete details concerning his early maritime experience. The Genoese merchant marine was involved in commercial navigation in virtually all parts of the Mediterranean and in the island countries of the North Atlantic, and we may presume that he travelled widely. According to his son's biography he visited the waters of "Tile" (probably *ultima Thule,* or modern Iceland, thought of as the farthest outpost of the known world) in 1467. That is the single documented date in Columbus's life until he went to Spain in 1485.

It seems clear that already as a young man Columbus had begun to project a plan to reach the Orient—often called simply India or the Indies by Europeans—by sailing westward. This plan was suggested to him, according to the account of his life written by his son Fernando, by his reading, by the exercise of his own rational powers, and by the experiences on the Ocean Sea recounted by other mariners. This implies that the project was less original than has often been maintained, but the question of its originality, like that of a possibly prior Scandinavian voyage to America, is essentially academic. The great originality of Columbus was to organize a sufficient level of financial support for the venture, to impose the fact of its execution on the historical record, and to advertise its results in a fashion that forever altered the intellectual landscape of Europe.

The logical place to seek backing for such a plan in the 1470s was not Spain, but Portugal, and it was to Portugal that the young Columbus went, possibly as early as 1471. Portugal, the home of Henry the Navigator, was the great maritime innovator of the fifteenth century. The king of Portugal had established as a national naval goal the discovery of a commercial sailing route to the East. But the Portuguese plan, which eventually achieved a brilliant success in 1497 to 1498 under Vasco da Gama, was to sail south along the west coast of Africa. It is almost certain that during his years in Portugal Columbus would have sailed the African coast, coming into contact with the black peoples who were from the start to play such an important part in the migration to America; but the Portuguese, preoccupied with their own African agenda, could not be persuaded to entertain Columbus's radically different plan.

So next he went to Spain, in 1485, where almost immediately he began the search for patronage. During this period the Spanish monarchs, like the Portuguese, had pressing distractions of their own, especially the reconquest of Granada, the last center of Muslim power in Iberia. A review panel established by royal policy to inquire into the practicality of the plan came to a negative conclusion. In the dramatic series of ups and downs that have provided the romantic materials for so many novels, plays, and movies, Columbus's hopes dangled by a thread as he was reduced to near penury before being befriended by the influential Juan Pérez, OFM, who successfully recruited Queen Isabel to the cause. Funds were made available for the outfitting of the famous three-ship convoy that eventually sighted land somewhere in the Bahamas on October 12, 1492. Soon he reached Cuba and named the large island of Hispaniola (modern Haiti and the Dominican Republic) and visited numerous other islands. He found lush vegetation unlike anything he had ever seen in Europe, and he encountered men and women strange to him. Since he was sure he was in the Indies, imagined as islands off the coast of continental China, he called these people Indians. Thus was the first encounter of Europeans and Americans marked by a prophetic intellectual misprision.

Epistola de insulis nuper inventis [printed letter] [Christopher Columbus] Rome, 1493. Incunable Collection. Rare Book and Special Collections Division.

While homeward bound in mid-February 1493, Columbus wrote a brief report concerning his discoveries of "Islands of India beyond the Ganges." He describes the islands he acquired and named for the Spanish sovereigns, the lush flora and fauna, the natural resources, and the native peoples. He depicts the inhabitants, whom he calls Indians, as kind and timid, willing to do much for little, and ready to convert to Christianity. Intended as a public notice to announce his discoveries and to garner support for another voyage, multiple copies were probably sent off to high royal officials from Lisbon in mid-March 1493.

We know that the first edition of this Columbus letter, addressed to his friend Luís de Santángel, financial secretary to Fernando, was printed in Spanish in Barcelona in April 1493. Within a month a similar letter to the royal treasurer Gabriel Sánchez was translated into Latin by Leander de Cosco and published in Rome by Stephan Plannck. The preamble to the first Latin edition gives exclusive credit to Fernando of Aragon for supporting the expedition. Whether an inadvertent mistake or an intentional omission, Plannck brought out the necessary second or corrected edition, which acknowledged Isabel's support of the enterprise and made minor editorial modifications. It was this Latin letter that spread the news of discovery throughout Europe. Within four years the letter had been published in seven countries, and before 1500 seventeen editions had been printed in Latin, Italian, Spanish, and German, attesting to the potential impact of the fledgling printing industry on international communications.

The Library's copy of the corrected Latin edition of the letter is the foundation stone of its vast Americana collections. The Library also holds multiple copies of the 1494 Basel edition, which includes eight woodcuts, four of which are directly related to Columbus's contact with America.

Rosemary Fry Plakas

From one point of view Columbus's first voyage was a series of disappointments if not disasters. To be sure, his feat was one of considerable personal courage and impressive navigational competence. Yet he did not find gold or precious gems in abundance, let alone the gold-paved streets of the capital of the Great Khan. He wrecked one of his three ships and had to abandon much of its crew as settlers in a short-lived and doomed colony on Hispaniola. He barely made it back to Europe alive, and then barely avoided serious injury at the hands of the first Europeans he met there. But, though he did not realize it, he had been the European discoverer of vast lands unknown by Europeans and as yet unnamed by them, the lands of America.

Columbus, whose chief anxiety at the most dangerous moments of the nearly fatal return journey seems to have been the fear that the news of his discovery might never reach Europe, almost immediately published a letter in Latin "concerning the recently discovered islands" that was sent to the lettered European world. Columbus's account of his success initially made a great impression on his royal patrons, who honored their promises to reward him extravagantly with wealth and position. He would be "the Admiral of the Ocean Sea" and in a certain sense the lord of all the lands he had "discovered" or would "discover." Columbus made three more voyages to America, incrementally exploring the islands of the Antilles basin and eventually finding the coastline, so long elusive, of the continental mainland. He was established as the governor of Hispaniola. But Columbus was a miserable political leader; and he soon had to be removed by force from his position under humiliating circumstances. The Admiral of the Ocean Sea, the discoverer of the eastward passage to the Indies in 1492, was returned to Spain as a prisoner under indictment in 1500!

The final years of Christopher Columbus were spent in what must have been for him a cruel obscurity. The Enterprise of the Indies, as the project he had initiated came to be known, continued quite without him. In the aftermath of the voyage of 1492 Spain had immediately become the principal rival of Portugal in a fevered race for maritime exploration; and their rivalry was rationalized in 1494 by the Treaty of Tordesillas, which followed the Pope's decision, made with grandiose arrogance in 1493, to divide the world between the two great sea powers. But the humiliated Admiral was to play no further role in the great drama after his fourth and final voyage to America in 1502. He turned inward, meditating on the vanity of human wishes and working on his anthology of prophecies. Christopher Columbus died at Valladolid in Old Castile on May 20, 1506.

Certain features of Columbus's personality are particularly intriguing. So clearly does he exhibit the attitudes of an outsider that it has been suggested that he was a *converso,* a member of a Jewish family converted to Christianity through duress. This is probably not true, however, and his attitude of marginalization is more likely to have derived from his sense of being a foreigner of undistinguished family.

In fact Columbus was an intensely fervent Christian who had adopted many of the militant religious attitudes typical of the Spanish Christianity of that period. He was particularly influenced by the spirituality of the Franciscan Order, of which he was possibly a confraternal member. Millenial theories deriving from Joachim of Fiore and other medieval apocalyptic thinkers were widely entertained among the Spanish friars, and they eventually played a

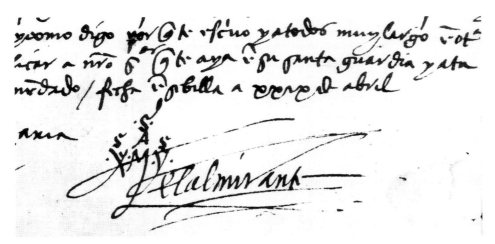

Columbus signature in letter to Diego Colón. Sevilla, 1498 [facsimile in *Documentos Colombinos en la Casa de Alba.* Madrid, 1987]. Rare Book and Special Collections Division.

Columbus's "official signature" has for centuries puzzled scholars. There is no general agreement concerning its meaning.

decisive role in the Franciscan conception of mission in the Valley of Mexico in the sixteenth century. Columbus came to believe that he had been called by God to a divine mission. He meditated upon his own given name, Christopher, which derives from a Greek word meaning "the Christ-bearer"; and the legend of St. Christopher, patron of travellers, told of how the saint had carried the Christ child across a body of water. At another level Columbus made a strong psychic identification with the Virgin Mary, a Christ-bearer of a different sort; and he insisted on naming his ship the *Santa Maria.*

He was a man of internal contrasts and perhaps contradictions, in whom a strong ascetic sense cohabited with naked appetites for gold and glory. A certain intellectual stubbornness, which in the aspect of perseverance accounted for much of his original success, kept him from ever recognizing that he had in fact visited lands wholly unknown to the Ptolemaic school of geographers. He went to his death insisting that he had found the westward path to India, and the land of the great Khan, and the fabulous island kingdom of Cipango. One of the features of his intellectual makeup that most surprises the modern scholar who encounters it is a certain inconsistency of mental criteria. Columbus had clearly mastered an impressive body of scientific knowledge, and his life and the lives of his sailors must have, on an almost daily basis, depended upon the accuracy of his meteorological and navigational observations. Yet the same mind that could calculate precise readings from compass and astrolabe was filled with the grossest superstitions and old wives' tales from the *Book of Marvels* of Jean de Mandeville and other extravagant fictions.

Despite its unresolved mysteries, Columbus's life is in many respects very well documented. His unquestionably authentic writings fill a good-sized book, and there are many dozens of surviving documents actually written in his own hand. His surviving writings include diaries, legal documents, public and personal letters, memoranda, and what is essentially a work of scholarship, the *Book of Prophecies.* We even have several books from his library liberally annotated with his marginal speculations.

Columbus lived at a time when Latin was in Europe still the universal language of learned intercourse, but when the vernacular languages were gaining ground in fields like law, science, technology, and even to a certain extent theology. Most of Columbus's surviving writings, all of which date from the later years of his life and the period of his public fame, are written in Castilian prose, not entirely without elegance but sufficiently leaden and

Columbus's Coat of Arms. In *Christopher Columbus, His Book of Privileges 1502.* **Facsimile. London, 1893. Harrisse Collection, Rare Book and Special Collections Division.**

As a reward for his successful voyage of discovery, the Spanish sovereigns granted Columbus the right to bear arms. According to the blazon specified in letters patent dated May 20, 1493, Columbus was to bear in the first and the second quarters the royal charges of Castile and León—the castle and the lion—but with different tinctures or colors. In the third quarter would be islands in a wavy sea, and in the fourth, the customary arms of his family.

The earliest graphic representation of Columbus's arms is found in his "Book of Privileges." Although the arms illustrated in the Veragua, Genoa, and Paris codices vary slightly in style and in color due to individual artists' renderings, they all consistently depict the significant modifications Columbus ordered by his own authority. In addition to the royal charges that were authorized in the top quarters, Columbus adopted the royal colors as well, added a continent among the islands in the third quarter, and for the fourth quarter borrowed five anchors in fess from the blazon of the Admiral of Castile. Since Columbus was not of noble origin, in the point he simply introduced for his family arms *a bend azure, a chief gules.* Extensive search of the relevant nobiliaries and armorial indexes has not identified the existence of such a blazon. Columbus's bold usurpation of the royal arms, as well as his choice of additional symbols, help to define his personality and his sense of the significance of his service to the Spanish monarchs.

Although the motto "For Castile and León, Columbus found a new world" is commonly associated with Columbus's arms, it was apparently introduced later by his descendants and is first mentioned by Oviedo in 1535.

The vibrancy of watercolors on vellum is well captured in this escutcheon frontispiece to the Paris copy of the "Book of Privileges," reproduced in elaborate facsimile by Benjamin Stevens in 1893, with transliteration and translation of the documents by George Barwick and an introduction by Henry Harrisse. This publication is part of a number of major documentary projects undertaken in Italy, Spain, and other European countries to commemorate the 400th anniversary of "discovery" in 1892.

Rosemary Fry Plakas

at times sufficiently faulty to suggest that that language was not his mother tongue. That, most presume, would have been a Genoese dialect, though his extant writings contain only a few lines of Italian. He also wrote Latin, at least to some limited extent and perhaps with some real competence. His letters are sprinkled with Latin phrases and quotations. He is probably the author of a brief Latin poem of the sort favored by humanistic schoolmasters, and there is no prima facie reason to deny his authorship of, or at least participation in, the famous and widely disseminated Latin letter announcing his discoveries.

In many ways the most important document concerning the biography of Christopher Columbus is also the most difficult to interpret with certainty. That is the diary kept by Columbus during his first voyage to America, a day-by-day record covering the events during the thirty weeks between Friday, August 3, 1492, when he set out from Palos and struck a westward course toward the Canary Islands and Friday, March 15, 1493, when he came to berth in that same port of origin. This record is unquestionably authentic in the sense that it does reflect Columbus's eye-witness account of his discoveries and of the first contacts between Europeans and Americans written virtually as the events it describes were transpiring. Yet it raises nearly as many questions as it answers, and it cannot simply be taken at face value as a straightforward account of the trip. We do not have the original manuscript of the log—a fact somewhat curious in itself, given the portentousness with which Columbus viewed his own enterprise and with which it was viewed by many others. What we have instead is a paraphrase and summary of the log written out by Bartolomé de Las Casas in his *History of the Indies* in the middle of the sixteenth century, some sixty years later. Bartolomé was a Dominican friar who has become famous in our time for his energetic writings in defense of the dignity and rights of native Americans, a concern already strongly articulated in his *History.* He gives no indication either of where he consulted the

Columbus bids farewell to the King and Queen. In *Nova Typis Transacta Navigatio*. Honorius Philoponus, 1621. Rare Book and Special Collections Division.

Within months after his arrival in Spain, Columbus had generated considerable interest in a return voyage to the Indies. A vastly larger expedition, with 17 ships and 1500 participants, left Spain in September 1493. Columbus remained in the Caribbean until 1496.

original document or of what became of it after he had used it. At times he stresses the fact that he is quoting the Admiral verbatim; but his awkward general practice is to reframe the narrative in the third person. "The Admiral says that such and such is to be found on this island . . ." "At this point the Admiral says that thus and so occurred . . ."

Bartolomé was a great admirer of Columbus. In fact, like the Admiral himself, he believed that God had chosen this man for a great and prophetic role in the history of the salvation of mankind. However, the friar-historian had his own polemical agenda, and he took every opportunity to stress the injustice of Spanish dealings with the native Americans. He does not hesitate to say of Columbus's kidnapping of Indians to take back to Europe that it was an act so unjust as to explain as divine retribution all the miseries and political reversals of Columbus's later life. There is good reason to suppose that the "edition" of Columbus's journal in the *History of the Indies* contains a good deal more of Las Casas than some scholars have supposed.

Another obstacle to our unqualified confidence in the journal lies in Columbus's own personality. He was after all a sailor of obscure but almost certainly humble origins. Amid the shifting alliances and petty snobberies and intrigues of Spanish court circles, he had every reason to feel the outsider. In his own eyes he found himself surrounded at the Spanish court by powerful but foolish people who were incapable of grasping the genius of his plan and too mean-spirited to work for its success. It is hardly surprising that we find in his actions evidence of a secretive, suspicious, and at times devious personality. The journal casually records the fact, for example, that in keeping the statistical record of the journey the Admiral "cooked the books" to make the sailors think they were considerably closer to Europe than they actually were. He tried to suppress from his fellow navigators the alarming phenomenon, which he seems to have been the first to encounter, of magnetic declination. These were hardly the gestures of the scrupulously disinterested historian of

Lunar eclipses, January 1504. In Johannes Regiomontanus. *Calendarium.* **Nuremberg, 1475. Rare Book and Special Collections Division.**

The knowledge of various natural phenomena aided serious navigators in the late fifteenth century. During Columbus's fourth voyage, in 1502–1504, his ships were beached for repairs on Jamaica. With the knowledge gleaned from Regiomontanus's writings about lunar eclipses, Columbus was able to gain favor with the local caciques.

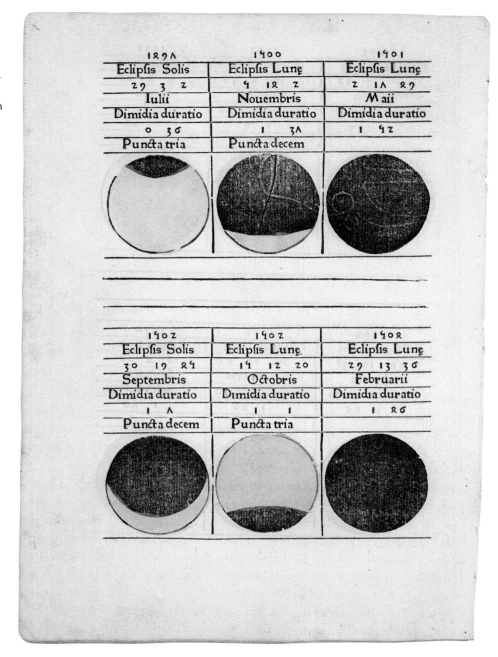

his own enterprise. The truth is that he was nearly obsessed by the desire to see the realization of his most extravagant dreams, and to see the world at large acknowledge that success. His wishful thinking almost certainly casts its shadow across the historical objectivity of his journal.

One of the greatest treasures in the Library of Congress is the Columbus Codex, a manuscript copy of the "Book of Privileges" of 1502. This is in effect a self-serving memorandum drawn up by Columbus in which he records all the promises of advancement, or "privileges," given to him by the Spanish monarchs. These included his being made a noble and his appointment to positions of high administrative authority over any lands he might discover. He had four copies of this document made and sent to various religious houses for safekeeping. Only the Library of Congress copy includes a transcription of the papal bull promulgated by Pope Alexander VI in 1493 concerning Col-

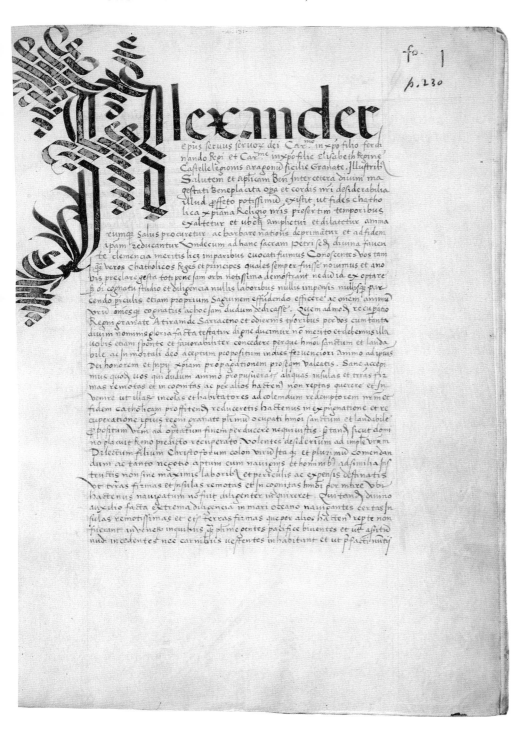

**First page. In [Christopher Columbus] [*Códice Diplomatico Columbo-Americano*] *Vellum. [Seville, ca. 1502]. Manuscript Division.*

On the evening of January 5, 1502, Columbus gathered at his house in Seville two local judges and three notaries, including his own, Martín Rodríguez, to authorize the preparation of authentic copies of his archival collection of original documents by which Isabel and Fernando had granted titles, revenues, powers, and privileges to him and his descendants. Columbus was then preparing to embark on his fourth and final voyage to America. Having already experienced the tenuous nature of royal promises that allowed his removal from Hispaniola in chains, Columbus hoped to protect his future interest in wealth and honors by placing authenticated copies of these documents in trusted hands.

The compilation of documents, popularly called Columbus's "Book of Privileges," includes the 1497 confirmation of the rights to titles and profits granted to the Admiral by the 1492 contract of Santa Fé and augmented in 1493 and 1494, as well as routine instructions and authorizations related to his third voyage. We know that four copies of his "Book of Privileges" existed in 1502, three written on vellum and one on paper. Columbus's agent Alonso Carvajal carried a paper copy, thought to be the Veragua Codex now in Seville, to Santo Domingo in February 1502. The Admiral sent two vellum copies by separate agents to Nicolò Oderigo, Genoese ambassador to the Spanish court. The third vellum copy, which was retained with the originals in the Columbus family archives in the monastery of Sancta María de las Cuevas in Seville, is thought to be the copy purchased by Edward Everett in Florence in 1818 and sold by his son William Everett to the Library of Congress in 1901.

All three vellum copies have thirty-six documents in common, including the Papal Bull *Inter caetera,* of May 4, 1493, defining the line of demarcation of future Spanish and Portuguese explorations, and specifically acknowledging Columbus's contributions. The bull is the first document on vellum in the Library's copy and the thirty-sixth document in the Genoa and the Paris codices. The Library copy does not have the elaborate rubricated title page, the vividly colored Columbus coat of arms, or the authenticating notarial signatures contained in the other copies.

However, the Library's copy does have a unique transcription on paper of the Papal

Bull *Dudum siquidem* of September 26, 1493, extending the Spanish donation. The bull is folded and addressed to the Spanish sovereigns.

This intriguing Library copy is the only major compilation of Columbus's privileges that has not received modern documentary editing. Comprehensive textual analysis and careful comparison with other known copies is essential to establishing its definitive place in Columbus scholarship.

Rosemary Fry Plakas

Further Reading

H. Harrisse, *Christopher Columbus, His Own Book of Privileges,* 1893, pp. xii-xx, xxxiii-xxxiv.

W. Eames, in J. B. Thacher, *Christopher Columbus,* 1903, 2:562–567.

F. Davenport, *American Historical Review,* 1909, 14:764–776.

A. Rumeu de Armas, *Nueva luz sobre las Capitulaciones de Santa Fé de 1492,* 1985, pp. 75–86.

umbus's discoveries. Of course Columbus's evident concern that the monarchs' extravagant promises might not be kept eventually proved to be justified.

Columbus's correspondents included the king and queen and other important figures, and many of his letters are very revealing of the religious and even mystical side of his nature which was not always apparent in his public career. In one letter, for example, he tells Fernando and Isabel that he undertook the project of the Indies as a way of recovering the Holy Land, and that he believes that his project was enabled by an inspired understanding of the Bible. In a legal document of *mayorazgo* or primogeniture, designed to establish the priority of his son Diego in inheriting his official titles and privileges, Columbus describes in some detail the famous coded signature, which has still not been adequately explained, which he used to sign many of the surviving documents. The *Book of Prophecies,* in which he invested much of the waning energy of his declining years, gives further evidence of an idiosyncratic religious mentality. By the end of his life Columbus had come to believe that his discoveries were part of a divine and "prophetic" scheme of history which had been predicted in a wide variety of sacred and secular texts, of which the *Book of Prophecies* was to be a kind of anthology.

Scholars will no doubt continue to search for the "historical Columbus" for many years to come. At the same time what might be called the "mythological Columbus" must remain an object of interest and investigation as well. For the figure of Christopher Columbus has played a decisive role in the way in which Americans have thought about themselves and their history. Columbus has given his name to a large country in South America, to the district in which the capital of the United States is located, and to cities, towns, and villages both north and south. In our own national history he has since colonial times been celebrated as an epic hero. The fashion in which Anglo-Saxon, Protestant America came to adopt as one of its principal culture heroes a medieval Catholic of Mediterranean extraction would be a subject worthy of an essay of its own. Columbus was celebrated in obscure works of poetry and music published in the first decades of the new republic. Washington Irving, one of the first American writers to gain an international reputation, wrote his biography and devoted other books to related topics. The life's work of the first truly great American historian, William Prescott, was his brilliant study of Spanish unification and colonial expansion in the reigns of the Catholic monarchs and Charles V.

Rather remarkably, given the fact that Columbus never laid eyes on, let alone set foot upon, any piece of what would become the mainland soil of the United States, he became an emblem of particular significance to the citizens of our young nation. In nineteenth-century popular American culture Columbus became an icon of the rugged individualist, the man who "sailed on" against the prejudices and fears of lesser contemporaries. Stories of the life and times of Columbus were staple fare in the readers of nineteenth-century American schoolchildren. Romantic fictions—such as the story that Queen Isabel pawned her jewels in order to equip his fleet—filled some of the many gaps in his actual biography. He became an emblem of intense ethnic and religious pride. Americans of Hispanic descent claimed him as a Spaniard. Americans of Italian descent claimed him as an Italian. The Knights of Columbus, the fellowship of Roman Catholic laymen, took him as their patron.

CHRISTOPHORO Colūbo zenoueſe hō de alta et procera ſtatura, roſſo de grande ꝫȝegno et ſa za longa, ſeguito molti zorni, meſi, et anni li Sermi Re de Spagna ī qualūche loco andauano, procurando lo ad uitaſſeno ad armar qlch nauilio, chl ſe offeriua trouar ꝑ ponēk iſule finitime ala ꝯdia, doue e copia de pie tre precioſe, ſpeciarie et oro, ch facilmēte ſe porria gſegr; Per molto tēpo, el Re et la regina, et tuti li primati d ſpagna, de gſto ſe ne pighaueno zocho. Pure tādem da poi ſette anni, et da poi molti trauagly de gſto colūbo, ſue al li ꝑpaſeteno et li armorono una naue et do carauelle, cu le ql acercali primi zorni de ſeptēbᵒ 1492 ſe parti dali lidi hiſpani et ꝯcomēzaⁿ el uiaȝo ſuo iſtituto da cadeſ ſene ando ale iſole fortunate ch al prite ſono chiamate da hiſpani le canarie nel mar oceano lontane dal preto 1200 milia ſerundo la ſua raſone che dicono 300 lige et ogni liga e miglia. ☙ Queſte canarie furono chiamate dali antiqui le iſole fortunate perla temperie del aere ch eſſe ſono ſtn habitate ꝑ eſſe al tuto fora del clima de la Europa uerſo meȝo di da gente riuda et ſenza alcuna religione: qui ando el colūbo per far aqua et tuor refreſcamti: prima chl ſe mehſſe a coſi dura fatica, deh ſeguendo ſemp el ſole occidēte nauigaⁿ 33 zorni gtinui et 33 noctr

Passage with description of Columbus. In Angelo Trevisan. *Storia de la navegacion de Colon* [*Trevisan Codex*] [Venice] **1503. Thacher Collection, Rare Book and Special Collections Division.**

Perhaps the earliest written description of Columbus is included in Angelo Trevisan's record of the first three voyages of Columbus and Cabral's 1500 landing on the Brazilian coast. Trevisan served as a representative of Venetian interests in Spain and compiled his *Storia* following their request.

As the four-hundredth anniversary of Columbus's voyage approached in 1892 there was a fairly serious attempt among some European churchmen to initiate a process of canonization. In 1893 there took place in Chicago the great Columbian Exposition, a kind of grandiose world fair in which the name and the idea of Columbus were optimistically associated with all the material progress and social and political enlightment for which Americans congratulated themselves.

The mood is very different as the country observes the Quincentenary of 1992. The past century gave birth to a number of less optimistic and flattering versions of Christopher Columbus. One celebrated Mexican historian found in him a typical money-grubbing merchant whose ideas could be best described by the adjective "boring." The most influential of contemporary Mexican novelists has recently published a satirical critique of the colonial mentality in which the figure of Columbus plays a complex allegorical role. For increasingly, and especially in Latin American countries, Columbus has come to symbolize for intellectuals the evils of colonialism and the European extirpation of the pre-Columbian Indian peoples and cultures of the Americas. For this reason the very idea of "celebrating" the anniversary of 1492 has seemed inappropriate, or worse, to many people. However we seek neither to celebrate nor to excoriate this complicated and still largely mysterious historical figure. Our aim has not been judgment, but understanding, and we hope at best to document some of what has been known or thought about Columbus and his crucial role in the complex encounter of peoples and ideas that is our larger subject. Whatever one concludes about Christopher Columbus, one can be certain that by the time the Sexcentenary is observed in 2092 new versions will have evolved of both the man and the myth.

THE COLUMBIAN VOYAGES—A TIMELINE

ca. 1451	Christopher Columbus (CC) born, probably in Genoa
ca. 1479	Marries Doña Felipa Perestrello e Moñiz in Lisbon, Portugal
1480	Son Diego born
1485	Doña Felipa Perestrello e Moñiz dies
1486	CC goes to Spain to meet with Queen Isabel in May
1488	Son Fernando born of union with Beatriz Enríquez de Arana
1492	Expulsion of Jews from Spain. Fall of Moorish center of Granada insures Reconquest of Spain by Christians

FIRST VOYAGE

1492

April 17	*Capitulaciones* signed with guarantees for CC
August 3	*Niña, Pinta,* and *Santa María* sail from Palos, Spain, with ninety crew members. CC is approximately forty years old.

August 12	Caravels arrive in Canary Islands for repairs
September 7	Leaves San Sebastian, Canary Islands, sailing due west
October 12	Landfall on Guanahani (renamed San Salvador). Area named the "Indies," the people "Indians." CC assumes he is near the coast of China
October 14	Departs San Salvador; visits Rum Cay, Long Island, Little Ragged Island
October 28	Arrives at Cuba; renames it Juana. Thinking it is China, sends messengers to talk to the emperor. Instead, observes novelty of tobacco smoking
December 6	Arrives in Haiti; names entire island Hispaniola
December 24	*Santa María* grounds off coast of Cape Haitien. Helped by Indians to save cargo, CC proceeds to build fort, called La Navidad and leaves forty-man garrison under Diego de Arana, Beatriz's brother; hopes to discover gold on island

1493

January 4	Departs La Navidad in *Niña*
January 16	CC sails from Samana Bay for Spain in *Niña* and *Pinta,* taking Arawak Indians as proof of landfall
February 13	*Niña* almost sinks in storm and is separated from *Pinta* in the Azores.
March 4	*Niña* arrives Lisbon; CC sees King João and sends letter "Insulis Inventis" to Spanish sovereigns; later this is printed and word spreads throughout Europe
March 15	*Niña* and *Pinta* arrive at Palos. CC goes in mid-April to Barcelona to see queen and king; is confirmed title of Admiral of the Ocean Sea and Viceroy of the Indies

SECOND VOYAGE

September 25	Second voyage leaves Cádiz, with 1,000 crewmen and 17 ships
November 3	Landfall at Dominica, sailing through Leeward Islands
November 27	Arrives at La Navidad; finds fort empty and no survivors

1494

| *January 2* | Establishes city of La Isabella under direction of brother Diego |
| *April 24–September 29* | Leaves La Isabella; visits Haiti, explores Jamaica and southern coast of Cuba |

1495

| *February 24* | Part of fleet returns to Spain; CC remains, further explores Hispaniola |

1496

June 11	CC returns to Spain, landing at Cádiz
July 20	Presents proposal for Third Voyage

1497

CC spends most of year at Las Cuevas Monastery in Seville

THIRD VOYAGE

1498

May 30	Departs from Sanlúcar, Spain, with six caravels
July 31	Lands on Trinidad; explores coast of Venezuela calling it "an Other World"
August 13	Sites Tobago, Grenada, Margarita
Fall	Trouble seething in Hispaniola with Roldán rebellion

1500

August 23	Crown sends Francisco de Bobadilla to restore order; CC and his brothers arrested, put in chains, and sent to Spain
December 12–17	CC is released; sees queen and king in Granada

1501

July–December	CC seeks restitution of privileges; assembles "Book of Privileges" in Seville
September 3	Nicolás de Ovando is sent as Governor of Hispaniola with fleet of 30 ships and 1,500 colonists

FOURTH VOYAGE

1502

April 3	Fleet of four ships sails from Seville on fourth and final trip to America. Son Fernando, thirteen, on board; later writes account of voyage
July 30, 1502– May 1, 1503	Ships explore eastern coast of Central America; in Honduras, Nicaragua, Costa Rica and Panamá, find many opportunities for trade, not for settlement

1503

June 25, 1503– June 29, 1504	CC marooned in Jamaica; stays one year. Captain Diego Méndez paddles dugout canoe to Hispaniola for help. Ovando denies assistance

1504

February 29   "Eclipse of moon trick" during Jamaica stay allows CC to secure food supplies

September 12   CC and 100 survivors depart Santo Domingo for Spain

November 7   Arrive Sanlúcar, Spain

November 26   Queen Isabel dies

1506

May 20   CC dies in Valladolid, Spain

...tomo e cucurcndiſſimo omnٓtuiu̅
...p̃ſ puepo tolciuo Karoinal
...manuſdpſinuur

Ira quoto
ritũ eorũ di
rtib⁹ ꝗ dit
t. Ego igit
lauera z chi
a parantur.
qui me ad
olico. A pro
habuit: ali
r̃ p̃ianoꝛuz
ni arbitrẽt
oite catholi
ninũ ita par
articeps im
erpers: hoc
a ingẽtes tur
unt. Chriſti
catores ꝗ ad
minãtuz viri
ludibria: ig̃
m nacti occa
ris negotia
cathenis car
tercꝗ omnia
anos oẽs au
rugoſa: naſo
it: et eã quaz
e fidei domuz
ne in dies co
n redimenda
maniſſimis z
iſtole calce re
is: ꝗ a primis
o religione ſen
mites ſtratas
cam exercitu:
ẽ licuiſſet. Sz
gis ac magis
ercludatur tã
poris eaſdem
renauigante
m hanc ex iti
ipſe viua vo
laturus: felici
nas Aprilis.

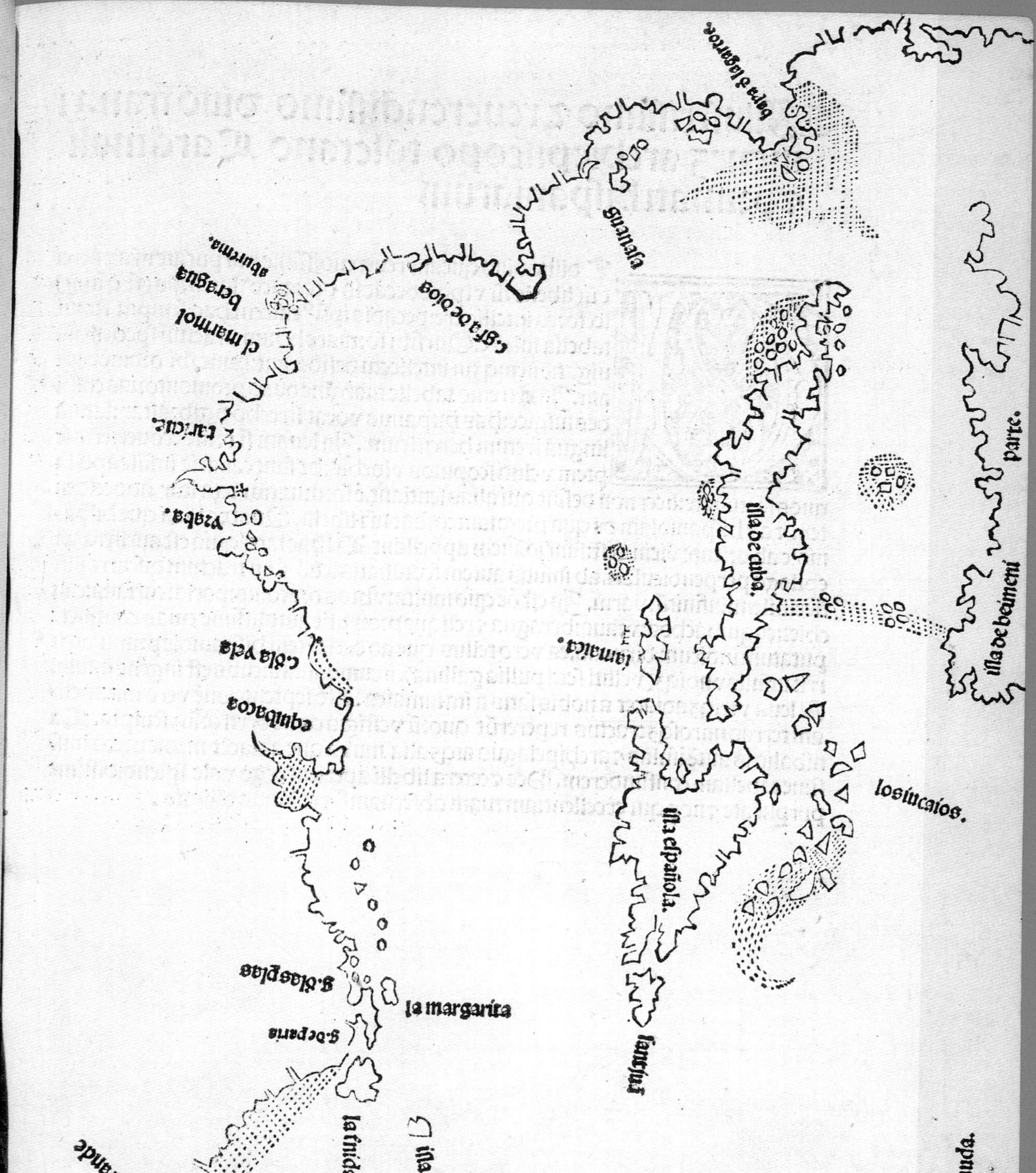

parias las bocas

ſiguana

aburcma

peragua

el marmol

tararc

illa de cuba

yꝛaba

iamaica

c̃. la vela

equibacoa

illa de beimeni parte

losiucaios

illa eſpañola

fanctiu

g̃. las plas

la margarita

s̃. de paria

illa verde

la trinidad

c̃. de crus

q̃. grande

canarias

la bermuda

el eſtrecho

CHAPTER SEVEN

THE CONTACT OF CULTURES
IN AMERICA

by IDA ALTMAN

N 1492 COLUMBUS and the crews of his three ships, who were mostly people from southern Spain, made landfall in the Caribbean, somewhere in the Bahamas. From that time onward Europeans and the people living in the continents of the Western Hemisphere known to us as the Americas, North and South, came into permanent contact. Columbus thought he had reached the fringes of Asia, or India. Spaniards called these lands the "Indies," and all their inhabitants "Indians, " despite the often considerable differences among the groups they encountered.

The contact between Europeans and "Indians" took a number of forms. Sometimes Europeans were conquerors of the peoples and territories they found, sometimes they were wholly dependent on the aid and tolerance of the local inhabitants. Contact generated a variety of responses on both sides. The peoples of America at times greeted Europeans warmly. At the outset they sometimes viewed them as divine or at least spiritually powerful beings, although disillusionment set in with experiences of treachery or mistreatment at European hands. Others saw the newcomers simply as strangers and intruders, to be grudgingly tolerated at best and strongly resisted at worst. The differing responses depended as much on the circumstances and world view of indigenous groups as they did on European objectives and values. The process and results of contact reflected the complex interaction of many factors.

First Contact in the Caribbean

The large island of Hispaniola, today shared by the countries of Haiti (an indigenous name for the island) and the Dominican Republic, became the first site for permanent European settlement in America. For nearly twenty years Hispaniola remained the chief focus of European activity in the region. Occupation of the other large islands of Puerto Rico, Jamaica, and Cuba did not take place until the years 1508–11, and around the same time Spaniards established their first base on the mainland in Tierra Firme (the isthmian region of Panama).

Once founded, such settlements became springboards for further exploration, conquest, and colonization. Spaniards progressed in leapfrog fashion, from Hispaniola to the other islands and Panama, from Cuba to Mexico and Florida, and from central Mexico to northern Mexico and what is now the southwestern United States, from Panama to Peru on the west coast of South

Facing page: **Map of Caribbean showing South and Central America. In Pietro Martire d'Anghiera.** *P. Martyris angli mediolanensis opera, Legatio babylonica, oceani decas, poemata, epigrammate.* **1511. Thacher Collection, Rare Book and Special Collections Division.**

This Milanese humanist at the court of the Spanish crown was an enthusiastic popularizer of the immensity of America that was opening up before the Europeans. For him, America was a fulfillment of ancient prophecy and a promise for future life. By 1525 he reported to his friend Gaspare Contarini of Venice that the islands of Hispaniola, Cuba, and Jamaica contained a million persons or more at the time of Columbus, but then, due to cruel treatment, despair, or infanticide, there were almost none left.

Modo di fare il pane. In Girolamo Benzoni. *La Historia del Mondo nuovo.* Venetia, 1565. Rare Book and Special Collections Division.

Bread making in the Caribbean during the first European contact.

America, and from Peru south to Chile and east across the Andes to the Amazon region. Only the most remote areas were excluded from this trajectory and were reached independently: the Atlantic coast of South America by the Portuguese (Brazil) and by Spaniards coming directly from Spain (the Río de la Plata region and Paraguay), and eastern North America by the French and English.

In the seemingly idyllic setting of the Caribbean islands, the people known as Arawaks or Taínos greeted the European newcomers without fear and with some curiosity. The Taínos farmed and fished. They were closely related to people and cultures in the northern part of South America, where they had originated. On Hispaniola especially there were some large, multi-village political entities, but the basic unit of social and political life was the village governed by a cacique, the local headman or chieftain. Villages consisted of up to ten large houses built of poles, mats, and thatch in which fifty to one hundred people belonging to related families lived. The cacique lived separately and enjoyed certain other distinctions of rank. He had some rights to the labor of the people under his authority but collected tribute only in times of crisis for redistribution. Taíno society included people of high status who were distinguished from commoners and also *naborías,* who lived in a dependent status.

The island peoples were known for their fine woodworking and woven hammocks. They used some gold, mainly for ornamentation, and knew some of the sources of the ore, although they did not mine it systematically. Although conflict among the Taínos was not unknown, they were not particularly warlike or very skilled in the use of weapons. Ceremonial ball games played by two opposing teams might have served as a substitute for warfare and an outlet for competition between villages and chiefdoms.

The other major group living in the Caribbean, the Caribs, were more aggressive than the Taínos and more effective fighters (Europeans would use the term Carib interchangeably with "cannibal," although there is no evidence that they practiced cannibalism). More recent migrants from South America, they were moving up the island chain. By the late fifteenth century the Caribs had occupied many of the smaller islands. They were maritime people who took to the sea in large dugout canoes that could hold fifty to a hundred people. The migrants who arrived in the islands and settled usually were men who would take Taíno wives. This intermingling of the two groups might have resulted in a fairly complete integration of Arawak and Carib languages and cultures had the arrival of the Europeans not curtailed forever the course of indigenous development in the region.

In order to sustain their venture, recoup investments, and repay borrowed money, Columbus and the other Europeans in the islands needed an export product that would yield a high profit but not be too bulky, since ships were small and slow. The only items found that fit these requirements were gold and, later, pearls. They tried first to barter for gold and then, as they extended their control over the islands, to exact it in tribute. Neither of these methods worked, as the islanders were not accustomed to producing gold in any quantity. Europeans then began to organize the production of gold them-

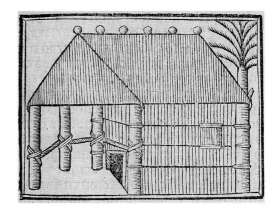

House. In Gonzalo Fernández de Oviedo y Valdés. *Corónica de las Indias: La Hystoria general y natural de las Indias.* **Salamanca, 1547. Rare Book and Special Collections Division.**

Oviedo's drawings of cultural objects in the Caribbean provide us with one of the earliest graphic records of American life at the point of contact with Europe.

Slaves making sugar. In Theodor de Bry. *Americae: Das Funffte Buch* **[Pt. 5]. Frankfurt am Mann [1595]. Rare Book and Special Collections Division.**

African slaves working in a sugar mill on Hispaniola reflects the results of transporting people from Africa to the Caribbean as the population of Indian peoples diminished drastically. Sugarcane cultivation was introduced to the Caribbean shortly after the initial voyage of Columbus.

selves. This decision shaped the subsequent course of relations between them and the Indians. The main thrust of early European efforts in the Caribbean was to ensure and maintain an adequate labor supply for mining and for agriculture, which supported the mining economy.

Spaniards used the labor of the islands' inhabitants in several ways. Before the end of the first decade on Hispaniola Spaniards who rebelled against

Columbus began to live among the Indians and divide up rights to the labor of specific groups or villages among themselves. From the time that Fray Nicolás de Ovando was sent by the Spanish crown as governor in 1502 these grants of labor were formally called *encomiendas* and their holders *encomenderos*. The people held in *encomiendas* were not slaves; they continued to live in their own villages and work their own lands. But the men often had to work in the gold mines for long periods, seriously disrupting family life and agriculture.

Outright enslavement also occurred from a very early time, although the crown quickly put a stop to the practice of exporting slaves to Spain. The doctrine of "just war" allowed Spaniards to enslave people who resisted conversion to Christianity, and many Indians were enslaved, branded, and sold on this justification. This formality was not always observed. Islands judged "useless" were virtually depopulated as their inhabitants were removed and taken to Hispaniola and other places to work. Frequently they called such people *naborías* rather than slaves, but they worked under much the same conditions.

The native population of the islands quickly began to decline as a result of mistreatment, starvation, slave raiding, flight to escape the harsh and alien regimen of work and forced relocation, and the introduction of European diseases to which the indigenous people had no immunity. By 1515 there were no more than thirty thousand Indian people remaining on Hispaniola. Gold production fell off, and the Spanish economy changed and retrenched. Europeans had introduced their livestock, crops, and fruit trees. Cattle ranching became a mainstay of the economy, and sugar cane cultivation got underway. Some African slaves were imported, mainly for the sugar estates, as early as 1502.

Despite the rather sudden end to the prosperity of the early years, a stable Spanish society took hold in the large islands. Santo Domingo, the capital of Hispaniola, became a true Spanish city. Built on a simple grid pattern centered on a main plaza—a plan that became standard throughout Spanish America—by the middle of the sixteenth century Santo Domingo had stone houses, a gothic cathedral, and a university, and it was the seat of the first high court, or *audiencia,* in America.

The Spaniards were not alone in the Caribbean for long. Other Europeans began to arrive in the region. By the 1540s English, French, and Portuguese ships were raiding and trading in and around the islands. English privateers and French corsairs attacked Spanish ports and ships; their forays were audacious and sometimes quite successful. But not until the seventeenth century did any other country establish a territorial foothold in the region. The Spaniards were remarkably successful in holding on to what they had and protecting the great fleets of ships that assembled in the islands after the conquest and settlement of the wealthy and populous regions of the mainland (see Chapter 8).

North America

In the sixteenth century, part of North America—the present-day United States and Canada—was home to hundreds of tribes speaking a striking variety of languages and dialects. These groups occupied distinctive habitats,

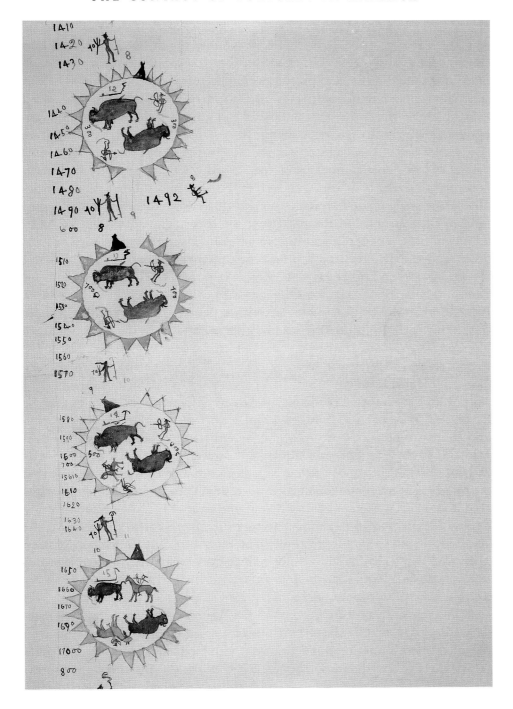

Winter Count, 1230–1907. Battiste Good, Dakota Chief. Manuscript Division.

Battiste Good was born Wa-po-ctaⁿ-xi (Brown Hat), during the year 1821–22. He belonged to the Sichangu nation, a Dakota-speaking people who are better known by the French rendering of their name, Brulé. Sichangu signifies "Burnt Thighs," in reference to a scathing prairie fire which afflicted part of the nation. The Upper Brulé lived along the banks of the Niobrara and the White and Bad (Teton) Rivers, until they were removed to the Rosebud Agency in 1878, after the war with the United States. It was on this reservation that Battiste Good copied his winter count onto sheets of a paper drawing book for Dr. William Corbusier, a U.S. army surgeon stationed at Camp Sheridan, Nebraska, in 1879–80. The meaning of the record was translated into English by the Rev. William J. Cleveland, a missionary at the agency, and summarily described by Mallery in the tenth Annual Report of the Bureau of Ethnology. In 1907, Battiste made another copy of the calendar, also on paper, which came into the hands of the Rev. Aaron Clark who donated it to the Library of Congress. This count spanned the years 1230–1907, although his earlier count began with the year 900.

Winter counts were used by the Brulé to mark significant events, each year (or "winter") of the calendar characterized by a memorable incident which occurred during the period of recording, such as the death of a leader, meteoric disturbances, fights with neighboring peoples, or seasons of plenty and want. The counts were kept and recorded by chosen men, generally elders, who were regarded as knowledgeable in important matters and the trusted custodians of history. The count keeper often passed his record down through his family, who added to it and periodically recopied it to insure preservation.

On ordinary winter counts, the years were titled, as in the "winter of the smallpox"–1818, but not numbered. However, Battiste's calendars included not only numbers but, on the Corbusier copy, English words as well. For this, Battiste has been criticized for creating a piece which reflected, in large part, his own accomplishments. His additions may have had much to do with the climate of Rosebud at the time, where missionary pressure to embrace English education included encouraging the creation of documentary records, supplying individuals with paper, pencils, and crayons,

from the Eastern woodlands to the grassy midwestern plains and arid southwest, and had strong ties to the land on which they lived. In some areas the subsistence base was fairly limited, but most of the people of these regions of North America derived a sufficient and satisfying diet from fishing, farming, hunting, and gathering.

These tribes of North America domesticated dogs, turkeys, and possibly other animals as well; took to the ocean, rivers, and streams in dugout or birch bark canoes; traded with one another—sometimes over long distances—for products such as buffalo robes, copper, turquoise, shells, paint, pottery, and food; wore clothes made of animal hides and of cotton, spun or

and (presumably) fostering the incorporation of English words as well.

The section shown depicts cycles of sixty years. In the period 1580–1640, horses were introduced among the Brulé—a result of the Spanish *entrada* into the Southeast and Southwest—and for the first time buffalo hunters were depicted both on foot and on horseback. The year 1492 also was noted.

Lee K. Miller

Facing page: **Carte geographique de la Nouvelle Franse . . . facit en 1612 [Fold-out map of New France]. In Samuel de Champlain. *Les Voyages du sieur Samuel de Champlain Xaintongeois*. Paris, 1613. Rare Book and Special Collections Division.**

The engraving is from the drawing made by Samuel de Champlain as a result of his voyages to New France. The figures depicted are Montagnais and Almouchiquas peoples; also shown are native plants and animals.

beaten bark, woven Spanish moss or other cloth; lived in houses built of wood and covered with mats, bark, mud, or whitewash, in multilevel dwellings constructed of stone and mud, and in easily transportable shelters made of poles and animal hides; and played games such as lacrosse and chunky. Their spiritual life and religious beliefs tied them to the land, to other living things, and to the spirits that animated and governed the world and helped to define them as distinctive peoples.

Europeans—French, Spanish, Portuguese, and English—arrived in this part of North America in the sixteenth century sporadically, in small numbers, and in pursuit of various objectives. Fishermen of all these nationalities plied their trade on and around the coast of Newfoundland from the beginning of the century. For the most part the fishermen and whalers of Newfoundland were not interested in colonization. They interacted with one another, and usually with the few local groups with whom they had contact, peacefully. Other Europeans—Jacques Cartier and Giovanni Verrazano for France, Martin Frobisher for England, and others—sought a "Northwest Passage" that would provide an alternative route to Asia. Spaniards penetrated this part of North America from the south—from the Caribbean into Florida, from Mexico into the southwest and plains region and the lower Pacific coast—looking for wealthy civilizations comparable to those they found in Mexico and Peru.

With the exception of the North Atlantic fishermen and whalers and the fur traders, none of these Europeans found what they sought in North America. There was no passage to Asia, nor were there great accumulated riches of gold and silver. The Europeans did not, however, confront an untamed wilderness. Instead they encountered populations that often were densely settled in villages and towns and found themselves among people who carefully managed and utilized the land and its plant and animal life. The Hurons of the Great Lakes region, for example, lived in semipermanent villages of eight hundred to sixteen hundred people. The men were skillful fishers. Women cultivated fields that produced not only most of their subsistence but also large surpluses of corn that the Hurons traded with other tribes for products such as tobacco, wampum, and furs.

The sixteenth-century European intruders into this part of North America were almost wholly dependent on the people who lived there and who provided them, sometimes under duress, with food and guides for their journeys. As they moved around they followed existing trails and trade routes. Making few if any serious attempts to establish settlements in the early years, the Europeans often made little impression on the people with whom they had contact. The most enduring impact of the expeditions of leaders such as Hernando de Soto in the Southeast and Vázquez de Coronado in the Southwest was twofold and entirely negative. The diseases they brought devastated native populations, sometimes spreading in advance of the Europeans themselves. Violence, deceit, and the wholesale commandeering of food supplies from people unaccustomed to, and often incapable of, providing much beyond their own annual subsistence needs disrupted indigenous life and left a legacy of fear and hostility. Some of the largest and militarily strongest groups, such as the Five Nations of the Iroquois and the Creeks, however, were able to dictate the terms of their relationship with Europeans for a long time.

La Terra de Hochelaga nella Nova Francia [Town of Hochelaga, Canada]. In Giovanni Battista Ramusio. *Terzo volume delle navigationi et viaggi nel quale si contegono le navigationi al mondo nuovo* [Venetia] 1556. Rare Book and Special Collections Division.

In the fall of 1535, Jacques Cartier sailed past the Gaspé, proceeded down the St. Lawrence, and moored his two longboats at the edge of an island in the river. Following a well-worn path through copious stands of oak and ground strewn with acorns and colored leaves, the Frenchman passed through expansive fields of corn in the midst of which stood the palisaded town of Hochelaga. The Agouhanna Donnaconna and other chief men at the neighboring town of Stadaconna had done all that they could to dissuade the proposed visitor, and yet, the Frenchmen would push down the St. Lawrence. Cartier would see Hochelaga.

Behind the three-tiered stockaded walls of the town rose Mt. Royal, the cornfields cloaking its lower slopes. Cartier approached the town in full armor, accompanied by four gentlemen and twenty men. However, midway along the path, his advance was checked, and he was made to rest beside a fire where there was delivered to him a reception speech by one of the chiefs, in what probably was the formalized method of greeting visitors. In turn, Cartier presented him with hatchets and knives, and a crucifix which he (Cartier did not trouble himself to record his name) was made to kiss. The Frenchmen were then allowed to proceed to the village, which Cartier described as follows:

> The village is circular and is completely enclosed by a wooden palisade in three tiers like a pyramid. The top one is built crosswise, the middle one perpendicular and the lowest one of strips of wood placed lengthwise. The whole is well joined and lashed after their manner, and is some two lances in height. There is only one gate and entrance to this village, and that can be barred up. Over this gate and in many places about the enclosure are species of galleries with ladders for mounting to them, which galleries are provided with rocks and stones for the defence and protection of the place. There are some fifty houses in this village, each about fifty or more paces in length, and twelve or fifteen in width, built completely of wood and covered in and bordered up with large pieces of the bark and rind of trees . . . which

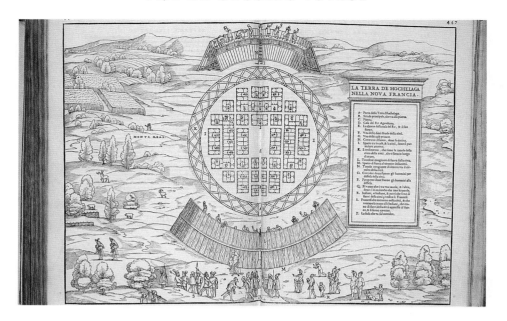

European activity in North America got underway with cod fishing conducted by Basque, French, and Portuguese fleets (English participation was limited until after the midsixteenth century) operating off the Newfoundland coast. The Beothuks of Newfoundland were fishers and hunters who apparently withdrew into the interior as European fishers, whalers, and fur traders became more active. Europeans did not really come into contact with Eskimos until the expedition of the Englishman Martin Frobisher in the late 1570s.

As early as 1502 Portuguese ships took back to Lisbon a substantial number of Beothuk men and women, and a Norman ship brought back seven Indian people with their canoes and other belongings in 1508; the latter people might have been Algonquians. Taking native inhabitants aboard ships and keeping them—to be shown as curiosities or sold as slaves in Europe, used as interpreters, or retained as hostages for future dealings with their tribes (or sometimes for a combination of these reasons)—early on became standard practice for Europeans who visited the shores and penetrated the rivers of this part of North America on sailing ships.

The next significant phase of European contact with the northeast began with the voyages in the mid-1530s of the Breton captain Jacques Cartier, who rounded Newfoundland and entered the St. Lawrence. Cartier met Iroquois who cultivated maize and came down to the sea for the fishing season. At the present-day site of Montreal, the French visited the palisaded town of Hochelaga. In the 1540s they attempted to found a colony at Quebec, but their presence in the area only became permanent in the early seventeenth century, with the expeditions of Samuel de Champlain. By the time Champlain arrived in 1603 the St. Lawrence Iroquois had virtually disappeared, and the French came into contact with the Algonquians.

The Iroquois, who occupied the territory from the Adirondack Mountains to the Great Lakes and in the seventeenth and eighteenth century would fight the French and their Huron allies, formed a highly effective political confederation by the late fifteenth century. There were five tribes or "nations" in this league (Mohawks, Oneidas, Onondagas, Cayugas, and Senecas). The affiliated villages agreed to ban blood revenge by an Iroquois against any member of the five tribes. The league provided stability, internal peace, and greater strength in dealing with neighbors and later with Europeans. Women played an important part in the political system, choosing the men who would represent the clans at village and tribal councils as well as the forty-nine chiefs who formed the ruling council of the Five Nations. The "Great Tree of Peace" symbolized the principles of the confederacy—peace and protection for all those who joined.

Spanish forays into this part of North America began early in the sixteenth century. Although undertaken intermittently and from different starting points, they were more or less constant up to the middle of the century. At that time attempts to settle and exploit the southwest all but ceased until the very end of the century with the expedition of Juan de Oñate and the arrival of the Franciscan missionaries. Activity in Florida, however, finally resulted in the founding of St. Augustine in 1565—meager results for a half-century of exploration and pillaging that alienated virtually all the Indian groups with whom they came into contact.

Juan Ponce de León, governor of the island of Puerto Rico, was the first Spaniard to organize an expedition to the Florida coast. Landing on the east coast of Florida in the vicinity of St. Augustine in 1513, the Spanish fought with Indian people—probably Timucuas—for reasons that are not known. The Spaniards might have thought a greeting party was approaching with hostile intentions. Eight years later Ponce de León returned, but the Spaniards were driven out; Ponce subsequently died of his wounds.

Two large nations living in Florida were the Timucuas of the northeast and Calusas of the southwest. Both groups built dugout canoes and lived in round thatched houses. They also used bows and arrows, and men wore penis shields. Timucua women wore skirts of woven Spanish moss; the men were heavily tattooed. Ornate statehouses with carved and brightly painted columns served as centers for Timucua political, social, and religious life. The Timucuas fished in weirs but were primarily farmers who cultivated maize, beans, and squash. In the mild Florida climate they could produce two crops of maize a year.

The Calusas were great fishermen who gathered shellfish, fished with nets and weirs, and pursued deep sea species such as dolphin and marlin. They also used their large ocean-going canoes for long-distance trade. The Calusa created artificial islands from oyster shells. One of their main ceremonial centers, Key Marco, was on such an island, surrounded by artificial lagoons. It had a large temple-statehouse set on a raised mound. Calusa chiefs were hereditary rulers with great authority.

Hernando de Soto, wealthy veteran of the conquest of Peru, undertook his expedition to Florida with the expressed intention of finding treasure, to be obtained by plundering Indian towns, temples, and gravesites. The expedition departed Cuba in 1539 and returned four years later, although Soto himself died in 1542. Immediately upon landing, the Spaniards provoked hostilities with the Indians. They proceeded to attack them, burn their villages, torture them for information about treasure, commandeer food stores, and take captives who were marched in chains as the expedition's porters. Moving north in the spring of 1540, the expedition crossed the Savannah River and was received by the queen of Cofitachequi, an important Creek town.

are well and cunningly lashed after their manner. And inside these houses are many rooms and chambers; and in the middle is a large space without a floor, where they light their fire . . . there are lofts in the upper part of their houses, where they store the corn of which they make their bread.

Upon his initial entry within the palisade, Cartier was met by a company of more than a thousand, and conducted to a seat of woven mats in the center of the village. There, people came to him making signs desiring to be touched. "[the women] crowded about us, rubbing our faces [and] arms . . . weeping for joy at the sight of us." Cartier, interpreting their behavior as a desire to be healed and as evidence of much suffering (not realizing that the act was part of the ceremonial weeping and rubbing of strangers—a practice widespread among eastern nations) proceeded to draw forth his Bible, and read aloud the Gospel of St. John, making the sign of the cross and praying that the people before him attain grace through baptism and redemption. Different in their systems of reality to the last, Cartier rose to take his leave before having partaken of food with his hosts—an insult within Iroquoian society. Accordingly, the women placed themselves in his way, bringing "fish, soups, beans, bread, and other dishes, in the hope of inducing us to partake of some refreshment and to eat with them. But as these provisions were not to our taste and had no savour of salt, we thanked them, making signs that we were in no need of refreshment."

This rendering of Hochelaga has received much attention and criticism for elements considered more stylistic than accurate. Part of the controversy stems from the disagreement over the provenance of Hochelaga itself and, although generally recognized as being Iroquoian, opinions differ over whether the people were Huron, one of the historic tribes of the Haudenosaunee Confederacy, a third tribe distinct from both, or proto-Iroquoian. By 1603, the date of Champlain's visit, Hochelaga (the site of present-day Montreal) had disappeared. Why this occurred, and where the population went, may never be known with certainty, although it may be that disruptions engendered by the European presence itself caused its destruction. The name "Hochelaga" has been translated variously as "Place of Beavers" (Oseraki), or "the out-pouring" (Osheaga), in reference to the nearby Lachine Rapids.

Lee K. Miller

From there the Spaniards went north into South Carolina and then across the Blue Ridge Mountains into Cherokee country. Along the southeastern rivers and their tributaries and on the natural levees of the lower Mississippi Valley the Indian tribes farmed fertile and well-drained lands that supported permanent village and town sites. Their principal crop was maize, but they cultivated and utilized a wide range of trees and plants. The cultures of this region reflected the legacy of the Mississippian and mound-building cultures, maintaining complex ceremonial and political centers and ceremonial ball courts.

The Spaniards everywhere abused their Indian hosts, taking captives and burning towns. Eventually they reached Arkansas and then started south again in the spring of 1542; Hernando de Soto died in May of that year near Natchez. Finally the expedition, having accomplished nothing beyond spreading terror, departed in July 1543, tattered, treasureless, and with about half the original group alive.

Timucua Dugouts and Typical Houses. Color facsimile of engravings in Theodor de Bry. In Charles de la Roncière. *La Floride française: Scènes de la Vie indiennes, peintes en 1564.* **Paris, 1928. Rare Book and Special Collections Division.**

This picture of a Timucua dugout canoe and a dwelling comes from drawings made by Jacques Le Moyne de Morgues, who accompanied a French expedition to Florida in 1564. De Bry made engravings from Le Moyne's drawings, which were later lost.

In the early 1560s the French attempted to found a Huguenot (Protestant) colony on the Florida coast. French relations with the Indians were poor, and the shaky enterprise faced a threat from the Spanish. They massacred several hundred Frenchmen; others escaped or were spared. French occupation of Florida effectively came to an end, and the Spanish established St. Augustine with its fort, San Carlos.

The Spaniards got along with the Indians of the area no better than the French; local groups attacked and destroyed much of the fort. Although the Spanish established a system of Jesuit and Franciscan missions up the coast as far as Guale territory in Georgia, Spanish-Indian relations continued to be hostile. In 1586 Englishmen Francis Drake and Martin Frobisher burned St. Augustine to the ground. Rebuilt a few years later, by the end of the century St. Augustine still was little more than a garrison of soldiers surrounded by unfriendly Indian tribes.

Hernando de Soto in the southeast probably had in mind his experience

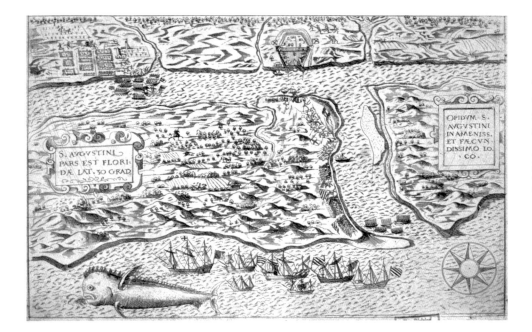

of the brutal but profitable pillaging in which he had taken part in Panama years before. Francisco Vázquez de Coronado, on the other hand, must have thought that the populous towns of the Pueblo Indians of New Mexico and eastern Arizona were like those of central Mexico. The Pueblo people lived in impressively constructed towns of multileveled and multiroomed houses, grew maize, beans, and squash for food and cotton for weaving, kept flocks of turkeys for their feathers, produced beautiful baskets and pottery, quarried and traded turquoise, and maintained contacts with their neighbors to the south.

In certain ways, however, the Pueblos were very different from the people Cortés had met in central Mexico. Pueblo groups had a long history of moving around in cycles of fragmentation and unification. In the early sixteenth century the competition for resources sharpened with the movement into the region of nomadic Athapaskan tribes, known generally as Apaches. Although the Pueblos and Apaches traded the products of farming and hunting, raiding and warfare were common as well. The Pueblo peoples' experience of conflict, their readiness to abandon town sites when necessary, and the limitations of the subsistence base in a semiarid land (which the Spaniards failed to recognize) made the task of reducing the Pueblos to obedience much more difficult than the Spaniards ever anticipated. In the sixteenth and seventeenth centuries they failed to impose effective rule, although their attempts to do so caused considerable destruction and duress.

Vásquez de Coronado departed Nueva Galicia in February 1540 and headed north into Sinaloa and Arizona, accompanied by hundreds of Mexican Indians as well as Spaniards. The Zuni pueblo of Hawikuh forbade the expeditionary force from entering. After a short battle the invaders took over the town and its food supplies. Elsewhere Spaniards repeated such actions, quartering themselves and their horses, sheep, and pigs in Indian towns, putting down resistance with great brutality. In the Rio Grande valley a dozen pueblos revolted during the winter of 1541.

Leaving the valley in the spring of that year Vásquez de Coronado and his force went north and then east into the plains, where they saw great herds

For thousands of years, the buffalo was an integral part of the Plains Indians tribes' daily life, figuring prominently in their diet, providing clothing and housing from the hides, and serving as a central figure in their religious ceremonies. To understand how completely the Indians put the carcasses of the animal to use one needs only to know that even parts of the bones were used for everything from weapons to cooking utensils.

Before Indians domesticated the large herds of wild horses that roamed the plains and that originated from the few ponies left behind by the Spanish conquistadores in the sixteenth century, the Indians relied on their ingenuity and knowledge of the buffaloes' habits and instincts in order to kill these mammoth beasts. In this illustration, the Indian hunters are using their understanding of the buffaloes' symbiotic relationship with the white wolves that populated the plains. The wolves would form packs to hunt down individual buffaloes that lagged behind the herd because of age or some infirmity, thereby maintaining the quality of the herd. The buffaloes were content to let a few wolves circulate among them as long as they outnumbered them. Here, Catlin depicts Indian hunters posing as white wolves in order to ensure that they could approach very near the herd without startling it before rising up and downing a buffalo with their arrows.

George Catlin was a self-taught U.S. artist who travelled by canoe 2,000 miles up the Missouri River to the upper plains during the late 1830s. He painted the Plains Indians before they had much contact with European settlers, allowing us to glimpse the Indian culture at a pivotal moment in history. Later, Catlin sold lithographed copies of some of his paintings that were bound into volumes entitled the *North American Indian Portfolio.* These informed the world about what he considered a noble and virtuous civilization that was endangered by the impending massive westward movement from the Eastern states.

James Gilreath

of buffalo and came into contact with hunting peoples. They also visited the lands of Caddoan tribes who farmed and hunted. As before, Vásquez de Coronado found no precious metals or treasure and no wealthy cities, although the plains people generally were friendly. In 1542 he was back in Mexico.

The last arena of significant European activity in this part of sixteenth-century North America was the mid-Atlantic coast. Spaniards went there, as they did to Florida, from the islands in the 1520s and, until the 1570s, made successive but ultimately futile attempts to establish a toehold on the coast. In the 1580s the English also tried to found a colony in the Carolinas. The European presence in the area did not become permanent, however, until 1607 with the creation of the English colony of Jamestown by Capt. John Smith in Powhatan territory. The Powhatan nation previously had experienced contact with Europeans, when Spaniards tried to plant a Jesuit mission on the York River in present-day Tidewater Virginia. The Spaniards were guided by a Powhatan man named Luís, who had been taken captive in the 1560s and traveled to Spain. It was Luís who led a group of warriors to attack and kill the missionaries in 1571.

After disastrous Spanish attempts to settle the mid-Atlantic coast, the Englishman Walter Raleigh was the next to try his luck. In 1584 he sent two reconnaissance ships which reached the Outer Banks of the Carolina coast. The English met Algonquian people there, farmers who, like the northern Algonquians, spent part of the year hunting. They also fished and traveled in dugout canoes. In 1585 Richard Grenville arrived on the Outer Banks with 600 men. He reached the main settlement of the Secotan, an Algonquian tribe, at the estuary of the Pamlico River. Despite having been hospitably received there, he destroyed a town and burned cultivated fields in retaliation for the ostensible theft of a silver cup. After depositing 100 men on Roanoke Island to begin building a fort there, Grenville set sail for England.

The English quickly wore out their welcome among the neighboring tribes, taking whatever food they needed since they neither fished nor farmed for themselves. The Englishmen used increasing violence to forestall what they thought was an attack planned by several tribes against them. When Francis Drake, bound for England in June 1586 after a privateering mission in the Spanish Caribbean, passed by the colony and offered the settlers a place on his ships, they accepted unanimously.

A new group of about a hundred settlers (including some women and children), with John White as governor, arrived the following year. White, who had been in Roanoke previously, returned with the ships to England for supplies, leaving behind colonists little more capable of fending for themselves or dealing with the Indian people than their predecessors had been. White did not return until 1590 to a colony once again abandoned. Possibly the people of nearby Croatan Island offered refuge to some of the English; but the fate of the members of the famous "Lost Colony" was never known for certain.

With the exception of the beleaguered settlement and fort at St. Augustine and a handful of Spanish missions in Florida and Georgia, at the end of the sixteenth century Europeans had established no permanent settlements in this part of North America, nor had they found riches to compensate them for the effort and manpower they expended in numerous voyages and expeditions. On the Atlantic coast, in Florida, and in the southwest they fought

with Indian tribes, usually precipitating the violence themselves. Only the French in Canada did not come into conflict with their Indian hosts, but they nonetheless unavoidably brought them the deadly gift of European diseases. It is hardly surprising, then, that when Europeans successfully established themselves on this part of the continent in the seventeenth century, relations with the Indian tribes became uneasy and frequently hostile. The two worlds—European and Indian—remained for the most part sharply separated and fundamentally at odds, notwithstanding alliances made for purposes of trade or war.

Brazil and Atlantic South America

The Atlantic side of South America, encompassing much of present-day Brazil, Argentina, Uruguay, and Paraguay, was home to as many as ten million people at the end of the fifteenth century. The populations of coastal areas and along river banks could be dense. The related Tupían-speaking groups of Brazil and Paraguay practiced slash-and-burn agriculture and lived in shifting village sites in which a number of families resided together in large houses. Hunting, fishing, and the collection of forest products were important, as were warfare and, among some groups, ritual cannibalism, although European observers in the sixteenth century probably exaggerated the extent of this practice. Groups such as the Tupinamba and Tupinikin typically fought people they called *Tapuyas* (savages), mobile hunters and gatherers who, at the time of contact, were being driven from the coastal regions. The Amazon region, which Europeans barely penetrated in the sixteenth century, was home not only to scattered groups of hunters and gatherers, as today, but also to agriculturalists. The Tupí-speaking Omaguas farmed and fished, raised turtles in pens for their meat and eggs, grew cotton for cloth, made pottery, and organized themselves into multivillage chiefdoms. Away from the rivers, in the dense forests, lived the hunting people of Amazonia.

In 1500 Portuguese ships under Pedro Alvares Cabral touched on the Brazilian coast, probably by accident. Following the example of Vasco da Gama, who had reached India in 1498, Cabral had sailed southwest of Africa

Facing page: **Indian village of Secotan. In Theodor de Bry.** *Americae pars decima.* **Openheim, 1619. Rare Book and Special Collections Division.**

John White, who went at least twice to the Carolina coast in the 1580s with Raleigh's ill-fated "Lost Colony," produced a series of drawings of the everyday life of the Indian societies of the area. His drawings are in the British Library. This one shows the layout and scenes from the village of Secotan, in which corn and sunflower cultivation appear, and domesticated deer roam in the woods.

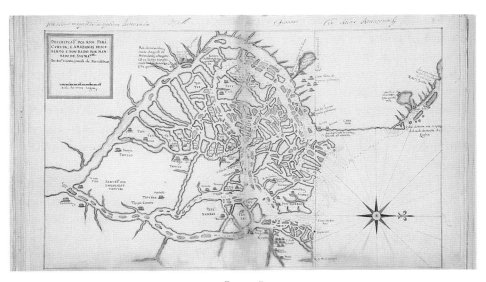

Descripção dos rios para, Curupa, a Amazonas. In João Teixeira. *Taboas geraes de toda a navegação divididas e emendades por Dom Ieronimo de Attayde.* **Manuscript atlas, 1630. Geography and Map Division.**

The Portuguese cartographer João Teixeira produced a rich collection of maps of places throughout the world in the early seventeenth century. This map of the mouth of the Amazon River provides a surprisingly accurate image of the delta region of that great river and the peoples who populated its shores.

Brazilwood, or "pau-brasil" in Portuguese, is "a dense, compact dyewood from any of various tropical trees whose extracts yield bright crimson and deep purple colours."[1] As Europeans soon found out, the dyes made from brazilwood were especially apt for textiles. Along with sugar (already known to Europeans and cultivated in Portugal and Spain) and tobacco, it lured Europeans to explore and settle the Atlantic coast region of northern South America in the sixteenth century. Thus, Brazil became a source of conflict and rivalry among the French, Portuguese, and Spanish who established colonies along the coast at various times during the sixteenth century.

In 1555 André Thevet, a Franciscan priest given to travel and adventure, sailed with a small group of Frenchmen under the command of Villegagnon to found a colony, a "southern" New France, on the Brazilian coast. Although he served as chaplain to the ecumenical group (there were Catholics as well as Protestants), Thevet's primary interest in the journey was probably fueled by an "insatiable curiosity" to learn as much as possible about the agriculture, customs, and language of the indigenous people of that region.[2] A curious mixture of personal observation, hearsay accounts, and fabrication served as the basis of his *Les Singularitez* of 1557 and of the later *Cosmographie universelle,* both of which were illustrated by black-and-white engravings of various quality and size. The *Cosmographie universelle* appears alternately random and encyclopedic. In the second volume, for instance, there are illustrations of contemporary European rulers, philosophers, ancient sites and graves, as well as representations of customs and occupations of indigenous groups in Brazil and their plants and fruit.

Lacking in scale and somewhat crude in execution, this illustration, nevertheless, gives some idea of the labor involved in the cutting down and transporting of Brazilwood to European ships on the coast, waiting eagerly to carry back their precious cargo. Thevet's description of this scene is noteworthy, for there is already present a vague awareness of European exploitation of an indigenous population: "But let's return to the subject of Brazilwood . . . When merchants get there, be they French, Spanish, or other Europeans . . . they trade with

in an attempt to round the Cape of Good Hope. In doing so he made landfall in Brazil. Portuguese activity in Brazil thus got started essentially as a sidelight to interests and commitments in Africa and Asia.

Given the orientation of the Portuguese empire toward Africa and the East, and the fact that Brazil apparently lacked the wealthy societies and precious metals that Spaniards found in Mexico and Peru, Portuguese involvement and interest in Brazil remained at a low level for many years. For the first thirty years after Cabral's landfall, in fact, Portugal made no real claim to the area. The only product of interest was brazilwood, which yielded a reddish-purple dye much in demand in Europe. The Portuguese involved in the trade supplied the local inhabitants with iron and steel axes to cut the logs. The Indian workers would transport the logs to Portuguese trading posts on the coast to be shipped off to Europe.

The French also were active in the brazilwood trade. Since they made a practice of going to live in the villages and forming close relations with the Indian peoples, the French traders overall might have been more successful in gaining allies than were the Portuguese. Some of the best early descriptions of the peoples of Brazil came from French travelers and observers. The French presence eventually became intolerable to the Portuguese crown, and the Portuguese destroyed the French colony ("Antarctic France") on Guanabara Bay in the 1560s. The bay became the site of the Portuguese town of Rio de Janeiro.

In 1532 formal Portuguese colonization began with the establishment of São Vicente, the first permanent European town in Brazil, located on the coast near present-day São Paulo. The Portuguese crown then launched a plan to settle and develop simultaneously fifteen captaincies along the coast. The donatary captaincy entailed a grant of lordship over a specified territory. The recipient had considerable powers of jurisdiction, taxation, and other privileges and could distribute land to settlers. The system had been used successfully to colonize the Atlantic islands of Madeira and the Azores. It was far too ambitious, however, given the magnitude of the undertaking.

There were some successes. One was the captaincy of Pernambuco in the northeast. Pernambuco for years had been a leading exporter of brazilwood, and the Portuguese there had allied with the major local group, the Tabajaras. One of the first areas to initiate sugar cultivation and import African slaves, by 1585 Pernambuco had a prosperous plantation economy with over sixty sugar mills in operation.

Despite the overall failure of the captaincy system, it did produce the beginnings of real colonization. In 1549 the crown sent Tomé de Sousa to Brazil as governor-general with orders to establish a capital, Salvador, at the Bay of All Saints (Bahia) in the northeast. The first Jesuits to arrive in Brazil accompanied him, as did royal officials, artisans, convicts, and other settlers. Portuguese Brazil remained a coastal entity. Almost all the main towns were ports, and the Portuguese barely penetrated into the interior. But by the latter part of the sixteenth century it had become a regularly constituted colony, with officials of government and church, a varied populace, and a profitable export economy.

The Jesuits played a pivotal role in colonial Brazil, maintaining close relations with the crown and its officials. In the sixteenth century especially they overshadowed not only the other regular orders but the bishops and secular clergy as well. Not bound by a vow of poverty like the Franciscans, the Jesuits went into sugar cultivation and cattle ranching with much success.

The Jesuits also had extensive dealings with the indigenous people and were Brazil's principal educators. Opponents of Indian slavery, they nonetheless felt that Brazil's inhabitants should be brought into Christian society. By the 1560s they were attempting to convince the Indian peoples to settle in their *aldeas,* where they would live under Jesuit authority. The Indian peoples not only received religious instruction, provided in a simplified form of Tupí called the *lingua geral,* but were expected to furnish wage labor for the colonists. Despite the protection they offered against enslavement, the Jesuits had difficulty in attracting people to the *aldeas.* Residents of the *aldeas* close to centers of Portuguese society were highly vulnerable to disease.

Epidemic disease took its toll on local populations, which began to decline; smallpox and measles swept the coast in the 1560s. The Portuguese nonetheless remained dependent on indigenous labor throughout the sixteenth century. They first attempted to barter for labor, then used force and outright enslavement. The Indians resisted the Europeans' demands. Barter did not function very well as an inducement to labor because the native Brazilians had limited interest in European goods. Routine agricultural labor in any case was considered to be women's work and, as such, was disdained by male warriors. European demands disrupted indigenous society and fostered continuing warfare, which also contributed to the reduction of coastal populations. To meet their needs for both skilled and unskilled labor, the Portuguese gradually began to import African slaves; but the use of indigenous labor and the enslavement of Indian people continued.

A high degree of indigenous influence and intermixture between Euro-

the savages [in order to get them] to cut down and carry the Brazilwood. The ships are sometimes a long distance from where they cut the wood, four or five leagues, and all the profit that these poor people get for such effort, is a miserable little shirt, or some other item of dress of little value. And I have drawn for you the figure [picture], as well as the tree, and the men who cut it down."[3]

Anthony Páez Mullan

Notes

1. *Encyclopaedia Britannica,* 15th ed., vol. 2, "Micropaedia Ready Reference," s.v. "brazilwood."

2. For more information about Thevet's travels and writings see Paul Gaffarel. Bibliographic notice to *Les Singularitez de la France antarctique.* Nouvelle édition by André Thevet (Paris: Maisonneuve et Cie., 1878), pp. v–xxxiii.

3. André Thevet. *La Cosmographie universelle d'André Thevet Cosmographe du Roy illustrée de diverses Figures des choses plus remarquables veues par l'Auteur, et incogneues de noz Anciens et Modernes* (Paris: Chez l'Huilier, 1575) 2:950, author's translation.

pean and Indian peoples characterized much of the European settlement of the Atlantic side of South America. The forms of political and social organization that would allow Europeans to superimpose their rule on already-existing structures for channeling goods and labor to the top that Spaniards found in central Mexico, Peru, or even the Caribbean did not exist among the Tupían peoples. Often they had to form close relationships—of marriage and kinship—with such people in order to take advantage of their productivity. The result of this intimacy was much greater indigenous influence than would be noted elsewhere.

The Spanish settlement of Paraguay was a good case in point. The colony there came into existence because of the failure of an expedition sent directly from Spain to establish a viable settlement at Buenos Aires on the Rio de la Plata. The Indians' initial welcome turned to hostility with the increasing demands of the Spaniards. In 1537 many of the survivors returned to Spain; several hundred continued up the river to the interior and founded Asunción, located in the midst of a large population of Tupían agriculturalists, the Guaraní. The Guaraní saw the Europeans as valuable allies against their traditional enemies, the nomadic hunters of the Chaco desert to the west, and they accepted them into Guaraní society, providing them wives and making them part of their kin groups. Society in Paraguay became increasingly mixed—mestizo—and Guaraní-speaking. Manioc, a tuber, was the staple food for everyone, as wheat would not grow in much of the region. The maté tea of the Guaraní became a successful commercial crop and a popular item of consumption in southern South America.

Throughout this region European settlement long remained tentative and minimal. The Jesuits would experience their greatest successes in creating mission settlements in areas such as Paraguay and Amazonia which attracted few other European colonists. Buenos Aires was not successfully established until 1580, and for many years it was a peripheral and unimportant Spanish outpost. Other parts of South America that were similarly remote from major centers of colonization and apparently lacking in rich resources—much of Chile and Venezuela, for example—also existed mostly on the margins of the Spanish empire.

The Contact of Cultures—Conclusions

We have considered here the circumstances and outcome of contact between Europeans and indigenous people in three regions of America—the Caribbean, part of North America, and Atlantic South America. At the time of contact each of these regions was internally varied, with people of diverse languages and life-styles occupying a range of habitats. The Caribbean was the most homogeneous of the three, but even there the largest political entities encompassed at most a number of villages. Europeans traveling through or attempting to colonize parts of these regions dealt with many separate and distinct groups and tribes. And many of these areas attracted more than one group of Europeans: the Spanish and French contended in Florida, the Spanish and English in the mid-Atlantic, and the Portuguese and French in Brazil.

One result of this diversity and fragmentation was the emergence of complicated alliances between Indian groups and Europeans; another was the

Différentes formes de huttes des sauvages breziliens [Brazilian huts]. Engraving. In Jean-Baptiste Debret. *Voyage pittoresque et historique au Bresil,* **Vol. 1. Paris, 1834–39. Rare Book and Special Collections Division.**

Debret's early nineteenth-century drawing of various housing types of the Brazilian Indian peoples provided an insight into their cultural differences and environmental factors that affected their selection of building materials and types of structure.

dependence of Europeans on the local people for their very survival, as everywhere in the sixteenth century they constituted tiny minorities, often at odds with one another. Yet this dependence did not necessarily foster relationships of mutual respect. Europeans often compensated for their lack of numbers by using force, treachery, and terror; and their unintentional introduction of diseases brought further devastation.

Indigenous societies survived nonetheless and adapted to the presence of Europeans in their midst. The plains Indian peoples of North America and Araucanians of southern Chile became remarkable horsemen; Iroquois participation in the fur trade brought them increased strength vis-à-vis their neighbors. At first groups usually welcomed Europeans and only later resisted them; but their response was not passive. They understood and pursued their own interests just as Europeans did theirs.

CHAPTER EIGHT

THE CENTRAL AREAS DURING AND AFTER THE CONQUEST

by JAMES LOCKHART

FTER MORE THAN twenty years of concentrating on the islands of the Caribbean, the Spaniards began their lightning conquests of Mexico and Peru, the great central areas of Western Hemispheric civilization. It is this phase that we primarily think of as "Conquest" and, indeed, it is at this point that one first hears much talk of conquests and conquerors among the people involved. From the longer perspective, we are perhaps not so interested in the military details as in the simple fact of the contact and encounter of isolated major segments of humanity. But it is significant that the form contact took was conquest, a phenomenon we can see across world history. In this process, a group invades another's territory and gains dominance by a combination of military force and negotiation, then settles in considerable numbers among the conquered for a long period, attempting to rule them, with lasting social and cultural effects. One example would be the Roman Conquest of Gaul and Iberia, another the Arab occupation of the southern Mediterranean including Spain, another the Norman French in England. The Spanish conquests fall within this context. And not only the Spaniards were familiar with the principles involved, but also the Indian peoples of the central areas, for in just the same manner their empires and confederations had taken shape, and they saw what was happening with the Spaniards in the same light.

In spectacular movements, the Spaniards gained control of the core of both central regions in a period encompassing under twenty years, and far less than that for the individual campaigns. Central Mexico was taken in the time from 1519 to 1521. The main events of the conquest of Peru took place from 1532 to 1534, though a great rebellion had to be put down in 1536 to 1537, and a group in remote mountain exile held out for a generation longer, without much affecting the course of developments in the main part of the country.

The groups of Spaniards carrying out these actions never amounted to more than a few hundred in one place, often under two hundred, whereas the Indian peoples numbered in the millions and were practiced in the arts of war, which were central to their polities and important in their social organization. From that day to this, outside observers have wondered how such a thing could happen. In discussing the indigenous people in pre-Conquest times, we have already seen the most basic reasons.

Facing page: **Conquest scene. In Fray Diego Durán. *La Historia antigua de la Nueva España* [early 19th-century manuscript facsimile of the 1585 original]. Peter Force Collection, Manuscript Division.**

The Mexica (Aztec) peoples confronted a powerful Spanish force supplemented by a sizable number of allies from the area surrounding Tenochtitlán during the 1519–1521 campaigns of Hernando Cortés. Durán's informants have skillfully distinguished Indian peoples from the European invaders, with a ghostly white image representing the Spanish.

First, since the Indian societies lacked steel for weapons and armor, they were at a severe military disadvantage, comparable to what most of the world faced in the late nineteenth century when Europe had repeating weapons and the rest did not. Just as numbers counted for little against a gatling gun, so there was little that native people could do, either offensively or defensively, against Spaniards equipped with steel swords and helmets, at least in a pitched battle on an open field. From the Spanish point of view, the greatest problem was fatigue from so much fighting and killing. Here the outsiders were served well by the horse, something else the Indians lacked. A few horsemen could push an attacking mass of Indian warriors back until the footmen were rested and could start over again. Under special conditions, which the Indians exploited when they could, as we will see, the Spaniards could lose their advantage, but normally they could count on victories even though vastly outnumbered, with relatively little loss of life on their own side. More Spaniards died in the Conquest years from disease and fighting among themselves than were killed by Indian attacks. Ironically, the people of the central areas were much easier for them to handle than the more mobile, scattered inhabitants of the rest of the Western Hemisphere, many of whom maintained armed resistance to the Spaniards and other Europeans for ecades or even centuries.

Second, since the indigenous peoples of the central areas, as we have seen, did not view themselves as a unified group, but identified instead with the many local ethnic kingdoms in which they lived, they had no inclination to band together against an invader from the outside. From their point of view, they were surrounded by outsiders, and their tendency was to see if they could find some arrangement with the newcomers that would help them against their traditional enemies. The tendency was all the stronger where imperial powers existed, and impressive empires dominated large parts of both areas. The first thought of each local kingdom was to use the new arrivals to rid themselves of tribute obligations and other duties to the empire. Thus the Spaniards would often encounter little active resistance to their entry; they might even be met with offers of help. It was above all those at the center of the empires, who profited most from them, together with their special friends and allies, who would normally put up a stubborn fight. The main rival of the imperial power was likely to be the greatest ally of the Spaniards; in Mexico this was the independent kingdom of Tlaxcala.

In the Caribbean the Spaniards had already learned about Indian rivalries and how to turn them to their advantage. They had also developed special techniques for first encounters, the most prominent of which was to get into a friendly parley with the ruler of the local kingdom (the cacique as they said, using the Arawak word) and then seize him, taking advantage of his powers to get what they wanted, at least during a transitional period. One of the most famous such episodes was the seizure of the "Aztec emperor" (i.e., the ruler of México Tenochtitlán) Montezuma (more properly Moteucçoma, "One who frowns like a lord"). But the same thing happened with the Inca ruler, and not because the conquerors of Peru were imitating those of Mexico, but because their actions were standard procedure, carried out scores if not hundreds of times wherever the Spaniards went.

The results of the Conquest campaigns were not brought about by any large-scale military organization or central planning and logistical support by

How the *Cazonci* and other lords tried to drown themselves. Ink and wash drawing. In Fray Jeronimo de Alcalá (?) *Relación de las ceremonias y ritos y población y gobierno de los indios de la provincia de Méchoacán* [Early 19th-century manuscript facsimile of the original, ca. 1540]. Peter Force Collection, Manuscript Division.

The conquests of Mesoamerica, especially in Mexico, brought drastic change to the inhabitants of the region. The shock of being confronted by forces whose weapons and military tactics proved superior to theirs, in addition to the political change that the conquests wrought, caused many former leaders to choose the path of those from Michoacán.

the Spanish nation state. The Spaniards in one new area organized themselves, with their own resources, to invade and conquer the next. The leaders were well-established figures in the base area, not quite at the top but anxious to be; they were responsible for most of the necessary investment in supplies and equipment. The ordinary members were mainly recent arrivals who had come too late to get the rewards their predecessors had claimed, and who therefore meant to be first in getting to the next place. They were not part of any permanent army, had no formal training or uniforms, got no regular pay, and did not even call themselves "soldiers" as most people do today, looking back at them in retrospect.

Whenever we get a chance to take a close look at one of these groups, they show a rich diversity. They came from all over Spain, from nearly every calling one can think of. Except for the lack of the highest nobility and of

Before the Spanish Conquest, the people of central Mexico provided tribute to their rulers in the form of products and services. These consisted primarily of corn and woven cotton cloth but could include such exotic items as gold, precious stones, dyes, or fragrances (see Francisco Lorenzana y Butrón, *Historia de Nueva España,* México, 1770). After 1521, within the newly established *encomienda* system, external tributes were no longer paid to Montezuma but to the conquistadores and to the Spanish crown.

By 1531, the conqueror Hernando Cortés had acquired dominion over far-reaching properties and *encomiendas* in Mexico and the titles of Governor of New Spain and *Marqués del Valle de Oaxaca,* which extended his power as far south as the present State of Oaxaca. After a lengthy absence from the region, he was asked by the people of the town of Huejotzingo (located in what is today the State of Puebla) to initiate a lawsuit against certain members of the first *Audiencia,* or high court of New Spain, concerning their burdensome utilization of the people and the unjust use of the incomes and profits secured from the town during his absence (see *The Harkness Collection in the Library of Congress, Manuscripts Concerning Mexico,* 1974). The legal case that ensued and the accompanying testimony—eight sheets of handsome indigenous drawings on native paper of maguey and *amate*—are known today as the *Huejotzingo Codex of 1531.*

Stemming from the frictions that arose between the conquistadores and the functionaries sent by Charles V to rule New Spain during the sixteenth century, this poignant and visually stimulating document reveals a highly stratified Nahuatl Indian social structure, with a complex and precise accounting system and an impressive diversity of crops, products, and professions. It contains one of the earliest known images of the Madonna and Child in these types of documents, a representation of a costly banner made of precious feathers and gold. The use of this highly revered form of indigenous artwork to display a Christian symbol introduced by the Iberian religious missionaries is striking testimony to the confluence of Spanish and Indian cultures and belief systems that was to occur later throughout America.

Spanish women (some of whom were often already at the base of operations), they were a functioning cross section of the Spanish society of the time. They were, in effect, immigrants, very much like immigrants to this country in quite recent times. Though they might return home if the conditions were right, they were prepared to stay if that was best for them, as many of them did. Thus Spanish activity in America did not take place in two well-differentiated stages, Conquest and settlement. Conquest already was settlement, and a permanent framework was set up during and immediately after the fighting.

The group of Spanish conquerors about whom we know the most is the party of 168 that captured the Inca ruler Atahuallpa at Cajamarca in north central Peru in November of 1532 in a parley-seizure that turned into a battle. They included numbers of notary clerks, businessmen, and artisans; some were literate, some illiterate, just as in the general Spanish population; some were modest gentry (hidalgos), some were ordinary middling folk, and some were from the lower edges of society. Perhaps a few examples will be helpful. There was Gerónimo de Aliaga from Segovia in Old Castile, a trained notary, who notarized wills, sales of horses, and the like, as the conquering expedition went from place to place. After the Conquest he became a great lobbyist and finagler, acquiring wealth and governmental positions that kept his family prominent in the country for centuries. Juan de Barbarán from Madrid was sharp with accounts and the management of affairs, especially keen on moneylending; he too was to establish a firm position for himself and his family in Peru. Gaspar de Marquina from the northern Basque country was still almost a boy, serving as a page to the leader of the expedition. He was illegitimate but had been given a good education, as we know from the colorful letter he wrote back to his father, sending money, telling his news, and greeting his relatives; he did not survive the Conquest. Martín Pizarro was from Extremaduran Trujillo, home of the family of that name that led the Conquest of Peru, though he was not their relative. Illiterate and from a family of shoemakers, he made a modest beginning in Peru but eventually became much respected in Lima, where he was frequently on the city council. Juan García, also from the Trujillo region, was often called Juan García *pregonero* (crier) to differentiate him from several other Juan Garcías in the group. He was a black, for it was a Spanish social stereotype that blacks should fill the position of crier. Juan García not only made announcements, he played the fife (another way of getting public attention), he held auctions, and he was the one who weighed out the great treasure of gold and silver the Spaniards collected in the aftermath of the events at Cajamarca. He was briefly a citizen of Cuzco, then went back to Spain.

On the Indian side of the encounter, unfortunately, the sources tell us little about individuals until a later time, and those are all rulers and leaders, seen with few exceptions through the filter of Spanish eyes and Spanish language. In some rare Nahuatl-language accounts of the fighting in México Tenochtitlán, the indigenous leaders seem to have stayed within their usual framework; at first, we are told, they were as much concerned with their internal rivalries and plots to gain the rulership as with combating the Spaniards.

After some reconnoitering voyages, the Conquest of Mexico started in earnest in 1519 when an expedition under Hernando Cortés came to land and

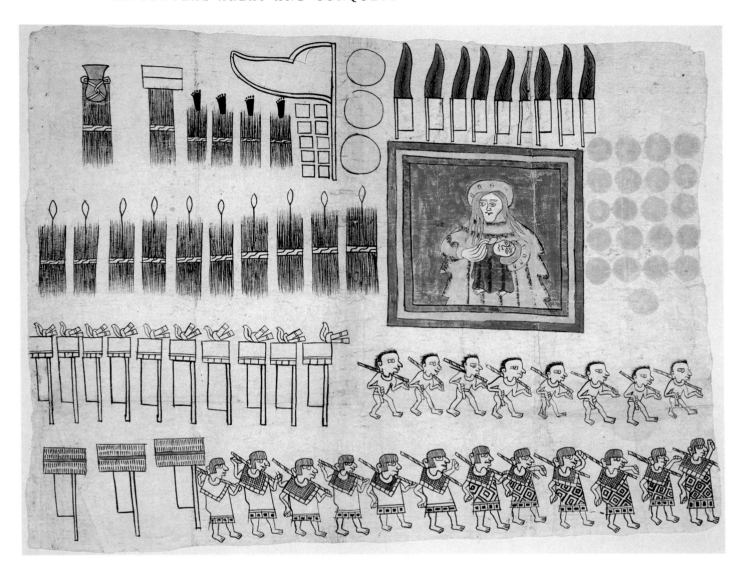

almost immediately founded the city that was to become the country's main Atlantic port, Veracruz. Everyone today has heard of Cortés, partly because he was well educated and articulate in writing. But he was in most ways a standard expedition leader: a person of long experience in Cuba, the base of operations; wealthy; the main rival of the governor of Cuba, who for that reason alone was happy to see him go and even to help him.

The kingdoms of the coast, which had only recently been incorporated into the empire of the Mexica, received the Spaniards peacefully and seemed to accept their rule. The powerful independent kingdom of Tlaxcala tested the newcomers in serious battle for a while, but soon let them enter and began to encourage them to march against Tenochtitlán, giving them all possible support and accompanying them. Most of the groups on the Spaniards' route seemed to accept them as the people of the coast had done, though some of the relatives and allies of the Mexica were of a different mind, and many of them actually went to Tenochtitlán to stay for the time being.

Tenochtitlán itself offered no open resistance; when the newcomers approached, Montezuma greeted them politely and housed them in his palace complex. Shortly thereafter, using their favorite technique, they made him

Formerly known as the *Codex Monteleone,* it was given to the Library of Congress in 1928 as a part of the Harkness Collection. Extensive conservation work has been completed on the eight sheets of handmade renderings which reveals the skilled production of pre-European paper and the durability of the vibrant inks the Nahuas crafted from natural dyes. Produced only ten years after the Conquest, it is a valuable document for a deeper understanding of the dramatic transitions that took place during Mexico's early colonial period. It also offers an opportunity to better appreciate the complexity and richness of the precontact societies with whom the Europeans interacted.

Barbara M. Loste

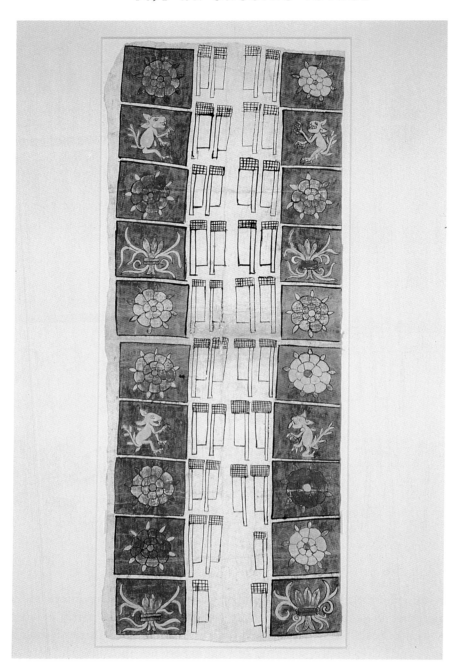

Cloth with designs. Amate paper. *Huejotzingo Codex.* **1531. Harkness Collection, Manuscript Division.**

The colorful designs and intricate weaving techniques of the peoples of the community of Huejotzingo, in the Puebla region of Mexico, are evident in this historical document. This sheet of the eight-page codex itemizes the variety and the quantity of woven materials that were provided in tribute to the Spanish administration in New Spain.

their prisoner and began to try to dominate the kingdom through him. Resentment and resistance, to both Montezuma and the Spaniards, soon began to show itself, as it usually did in these cases; the seized cacique rarely survived for very long. He was likely to be killed by the Spaniards as useless and uncooperative, or by the Indian people as a traitor. In Montezuma's case, we are not entirely sure which of the two elements accounted for his early death. In any event, Cortés having gone back to the coast to face the challenge of a new expedition from Cuba, the Spaniards in Tenochtitlán were soon under siege, as Cortés found them on his return (he overcame the challenge handily, for Spaniards always readily acknowledged the rights of whoever got to an area first).

How is it, we might ask, that the Spaniards found themselves in such straits, given their vastly superior swords, helmets, and horses? For these assets to be brought to bear, a certain amount of open space was needed. Tenochtitlán was the worst situation for battle that the Spaniards could have imagined: on an island in a great lake, approachable only through a few causeways, crisscrossed with deep canals, densely covered with fortresslike buildings and walls. There was no alternative to a Spanish retreat, an attempt to get out of the city by night, but in crossing the canals the Spaniards and their allies the Tlaxcalans lost both people and equipment on a large scale. Some did survive, however, and nothing could be more telling about the nature of the underlying situation than the fact that in a sad state of fatigue and low morale, after all their losses, the Spaniards gained the victory in a battle on open fields at Otumba, northeast of Tenochtitlán.

They retreated to Tlaxcala to regroup, however, returning after an interval of many months with more newly arrived Spaniards and a small fleet of brigantines built in Tlaxcala in order to dominate the lake and make a siege possible. A siege and assault on the city then ensued, without parallel in the history of the Indies. Even with their now numerous Indian allies, the Spaniards could accomplish little with their ordinary methods. If they fought their way laboriously down narrow causeways and into the city, when they came back the next day they would have to do the whole thing over again. In due course they began knocking down buildings and filling in canals in the portions they had won, creating bit by bit the open field they needed, and in this way, with the help of famine and smallpox among the besieged, they finally induced the Mexica to surrender (1521).

The central Mexican conquest is exceptional not only in the nature of the fighting at Tenochtitlán but in the fact that we have some accounts of it written from the Indian point of view. All of them, though, are from Tenochtitlán itself or from groups closely associated with it. Other histories of central Mexican city states tend to play down or ignore the Conquest, as though it hardly mattered whether the Spaniards or the Mexica were the imperial

Montezuma awaits Cortés. In Fray Diego Durán. *La Historia antigua de la Nueva España* **[Early 19th-century manuscript facsimile of the 1585 original]. Peter Force Collection, Manuscript Division.**

The leader of the Mexica (Aztec) peoples had learned of the newcomers who arrived on the Gulf coastal shores near Veracruz. He was convinced that their arrival spelled doom for himself and his empire.

Facing page: **The Oztoticpac Lands Map.
Amate paper, ca. 1540. Geography and
Map Division.**

Picture writing on manuscripts of *amate*
paper or on animal skin is of unknown antiquity in Mesoamerica, although it substantially predates the arrival of the Europeans. Following the Spanish Conquest in
Mexico in the first quarter of the sixteenth
century, painted manuscripts in various native artistic traditions continued to be produced, particularly in central Mexico and
Oaxaca. In civil and economic matters Indian peoples and Spaniards alike found
that maps, tribute registers, and cadastral
and census documents derived from native
traditions met a common need.

The survival of a significant corpus of
manuscript drawings from both ancient and
colonial Mesoamerica provides archaeolo-
gists and ethnohistorians a unique body of
American material sources. Research into
the full meaning of documents such as the
Oztoticpac Lands Map continues as modern scholars attempt to unlock the rich and
mysterious history of pre-European cultures
in America and their reactions to the newcomers.

The Oztoticpac (Mexico) Lands Map is a
central Mexican pictorial document with
Spanish and Nahuatl writing showing litigation surrounding the Oztoticpac estate
within the city of Texcoco, ca. 1540. Its
glyph, a symbolic figure, corresponds to the
name "above the caves" (*oztotl,* cave; *icpac,*
above), a hill stylized in the shape of a
woman. The document on pre-European
amate paper involves the land and property
ownership of the ruler of Texcoco who was
executed during the early days of the Spanish Conquest in the Central Valley of Mexico. The execution left in its wake litigation
involving ownership of properties claimed
by various sons of Nezahualpilli, the lords
of Texcoco.

The major protagonist, Don Carlos
Ometochtli Chichimecatecotl, was executed
by Spanish officials on November 30, 1539,
in the public square of Mexico City. He had
been convicted by the Inquisition for hereti-
cal dogmatizing, idolatry, and immorality.
The execution of one of the powerful lords
of Texcoco, for whatever reasons, was a
critical event. It damaged the prestige of
the Inquisitor Bishop Juan Zumárraga, who
was officially reprimanded for his action.

Most of the drawings on the map are
plans of fields with indigenous measure-
ments and place glyphs. Near the upper left
is the plan of several houses within a pre-

power. It was the Mexica themselves who were most directly affected, who
had the most vivid memories, and who wrote them down afterward.

The largest of these accounts falls into two parts. The first consists of
legends built up in the thirty or more years before anything was written
down. Various kinds of explanations are given for what happened. One is fate;
a set of eight omens is listed, supposedly foreshadowing the doom of the
Mexica. Another is the identification of a scapegoat: an indecisive, cowardly,
superstitious Montezuma who brought about his own downfall (not to speak
of his earlier arrogance toward his own people). Another is the alleged belief
that the man-god Quetzalcoatl, who had once disappeared into the eastern
ocean promising to return to rule, was embodied in Hernando Cortés. The
first two are common responses of any group which has suffered a disaster.
The third is harder to evaluate, but recent scholarship tends to show that the
myth of the returning Quetzalcoatl grew up gradually over the two generations following contact and was not an important factor in the reaction of the
indigenous people actually involved.

A second part of the account is devoted to telling, at times almost day
by day, the events that took place in Tenochtitlán. It gives every evidence of
resting on authentic oral tradition carried down faithfully from the time of
the events. It concentrates overwhelmingly on the Mexica themselves, with
little concern about what happened outside Tenochtitlán and the immediate
environs. "We" are the Mexica; "they" are the Spaniards and the other Indian
groups, and the frequently used category "our enemies" includes both. The
Mexica adjust pragmatically to the methods the Spaniards use, soon learning
to hit the ground and disperse when the cannon are fired, and so on. They tell
of their successes and defeats matter-of-factly, with little condemnation of
anyone, though also with a great sense of pride in their corporate accomplishments.

It is noteworthy not only that the account never speaks of "Indians" but
that it emphasizes ethnic and political distinctions even among the defenders
on the island. Early in their existence, the Mexica had split into two parallel
entities, of which the senior was Tenochtitlán proper, occupying the southern
part of the island, and the junior was Tlatelolco, occupying the northern part.
The account happens to be written by Tlatelolca (inhabitants of Tlatelolco),
who were at pains to show that everything was done equally by the two parts
(though in fact Tenochtitlán was much larger and overwhelmingly dominant). The full fury of the Spanish onslaught was directed first against Tenochtitlán proper, and when that section had been virtually destroyed, the
Tenochca naturally enough took refuge in Tlatelolco. But the Tlatelolca ac-
cuse them of cowardice, say that they should have defended their part as well
as the Tlatelolca did theirs, and make other cutting remarks. Even in the
imperial centers, during the fighting and for generations afterward, mi-
croethnic pride ruled supreme. From the point of view of the Indian chroniclers, the world was not utterly transformed merely because some Spaniards
had arrived and made their presence mightily felt.

Let us not go into such detail with the Peruvian conquest. We have
already talked of the nature of the group of Spaniards involved. Their leader,
Francisco Pizarro, was the usual senior and wealthy figure of good family
(though he happened to be an illegitimate member of that family and had
received no formal education). The Inca empire was just reaching the end of

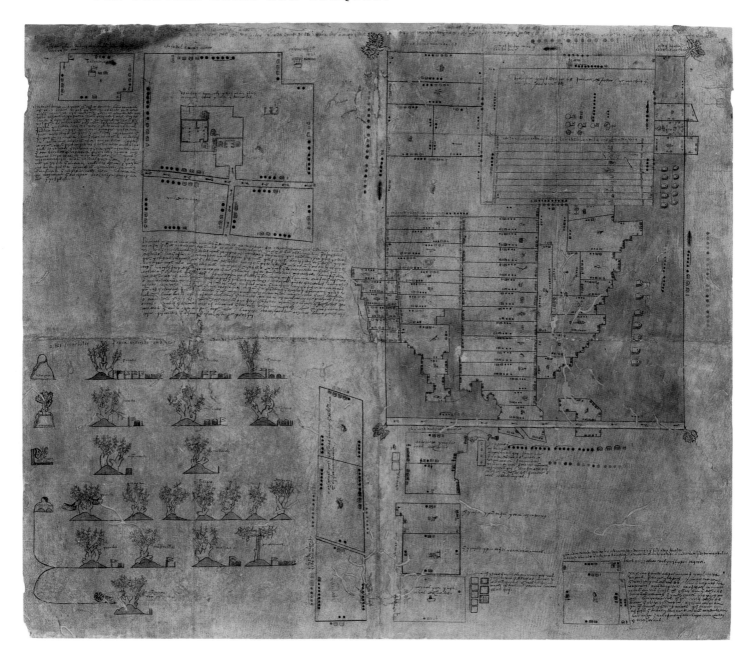

cinct. On the upper right is a map showing about seventy-five plots of land. Additional fields are drawn at the lower right. Nahuatl and Spanish descriptions as well as three long Nahuatl texts include mention of Tol-lancingo, Oztoticpac, Tezcuco, Don Carlos, and Don Hernando.

In the lower left of the map are depictions of tree grafts, showing European fruit tree branches grafted to indigenous tree trunks, uniquely displayed among all known Mexican Indian pictorial documents. Twenty trees, identified as pomegranates, quinces, apples, pears, etc., are shown. Also, as far as it is known, this is the earliest recorded lawsuit or conflict in horticultural literature anywhere in the world.

Substantial introductory work on the rare pictorial manuscript was provided by Howard F. Cline in "The Oztoticpac Lands Map of Texcoco, 1540," *Quarterly Journal of the Library of Congress,* 23:76–115 (April 1966). In that detailed article Cline provides the initial interpretation of the various segments of the map and the historical context of the document. His preliminary studies revealed it to be a complicated mystery. He felt that its closing scene remained to be written when data now lying in unplumbed archives became available.

John R. Hébert

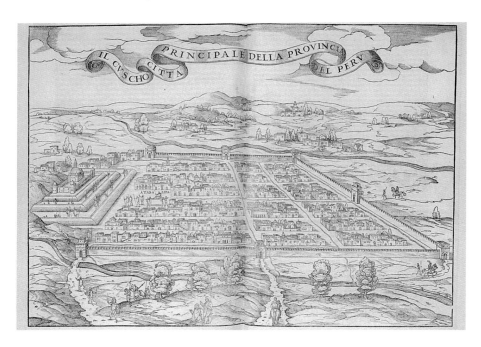

Il Cuscho Cita Principale Della Provincia Del Peru [Cuzco]. In Giovanni Battista Ramusio. *Terzo volume delle navigationi et viaggi nel quale si contengono le navigationi al mondo nuovo.* **[Venetia] 1556. Rare Book and Special Collections Division.**

This principal city of the Incan empire in the Andes was constructed by more than thirty thousand laborers. It remained the center of Indian peoples' activities in Peru, as the Spanish conquerors established Lima closer to the Pacific Ocean.

a civil war when the Spaniards arrived, so that the current Inca ruler's hold was not well consolidated, and many groups were especially ready to accept the outsiders as deliverers. A series of brief encounters took place in the campaign of 1532 to 1534, but there was nothing comparable to the siege of Tenochtitlán. The greatest difficulty the Spaniards had was that of climbing twisting trails into the highlands, at which point they were highly vulnerable and sometimes lost whole parties to boulders and missiles hurled from above. After the core of the country had been occupied, a large-scale rebellion broke out. In 1536 to 1537 Indian societies rose throughout the central highlands and as far as the new coastal city of Lima, which they threatened. At Cuzco, their home base, they took control of the whole countryside and enclosed the some two hundred Spaniards who were present in the city proper. But for all their efforts, and despite the Spanish lack of numerous indigenous auxiliaries as in Mexico, few Spaniards were killed, and when an expedition to Chile returned, dissatisfied with what it had found, the two Spanish groups were able to regain the upper hand. From that time forward, the main problem for the Spaniards was internal strife, showing itself in a series of Spanish civil wars not ending until the early 1550s.

Nothing, however, held back the organization of a new system in both major areas, starting the moment the Spaniards arrived. We have seen the foundation of Veracruz in Mexico when the conquest had hardly begun; something similar happened with the foundation of Piura in Peru well before the events of Cajamarca. Other Spanish cities were established during or immediately after the fighting; each region had acquired its basic city network, much as it has existed ever since, in less than ten years after the end of large-scale hostilities. The distribution of the cities was not haphazard or the arbitrary decision of the Spaniards. If they had meant to start from scratch, they would have gone elsewhere. Their intention was to build on what already existed. Each city was to be a base out of which Spaniards could dominate and profit from a major area of Indian population. Thus the Spanish network tended to follow the indigenous settlement pattern, at times very closely.

Explorer on Llama. Title page. In Ulrich Schmidel. *Vera Historia . . . quam Huldericus Schmidel.* **Noribergae [Nuremberg], 1559. Rare Book and Special Collections Division.**

Europe's fascination with the tales regarding Incan gold and silver and other products led to a steady stream of explorers and merchants who sought ways to become a part of the economy.

In Mexico, the Spanish capital of Mexico City was built directly on what remained of Tenochtitlán, with the central square in the same place, the governmental palace where Montezuma's had been, and the cathedral on the site of the old temple complex. Around the Spanish center stretched Indian Tenochtitlán, still organized into the same districts as before the Conquest. The same thing happened in Cuzco, but the original plan of making it the Spanish capital did not come to pass. The extreme conditions of Andean geography and climate, which as we have seen brought about elaborate adaptations in indigenous society, showed their force once again. Cuzco was too hard for the Spaniards to reach, and the rigors of the Andean highlands were a strong deterrent. Leaving Cuzco as merely one city among others, they tried Jauja, farther to the north and at a somewhat lower altitude, as the capital, then soon gave that up too, and established Lima on the coast. The Mexican system (with the important addition of a port connecting the country with Europe) faithfully replicated what had been there before, and thus brought the bulk of the incoming Spaniards into quite direct contact with the bulk of the indigenous population. In Peru, the majority of the Spaniards were to be on the coast, the great majority of the Indian settlements in the highlands, leading to less cultural and racial mixing than in Mexico, with results that can be seen even today.

The cities the Spaniards set up can hardly be understood without consideration of an institution called the *encomienda*. The Spanish tradition, formed in the medieval reconquest of their country from the Moors, was to divide out newly occupied lands to those who occupied them. The *encomienda* was the form this tradition assumed in America; it involved assigning one of those local Indian kingdoms we have already discussed to one Spaniard, the *encomendero,* to provide him with whatever benefits normally accrued to its lord or overlord. In some areas this might be labor from the rotary draft system, in some it might be tribute in local products; in the central areas, the local kingdoms could provide both, and many of them were already used to giving tribute to an imperial power. The system involved retaining local units with their territories and authorities intact, which was precisely what those groups wanted. Nowhere in the central areas did the Spaniards have serious trouble in establishing the *encomienda* in principle; it soon became the main link between the indigenous population and the newcomers. A Spanish city was above all a concentration point for *encomenderos,* whose grants stretched across a vast district with the city at its center. The city was Spanish, the rest Indian.

Into the *encomenderos'* cities there soon flooded thousands of other Spanish people, quite a few women among the male majority, from all over Castile, from many different strata and occupations—professional people, merchants, craftsmen, managers, and others, all still prepared to practice those occupations if they were profitable enough. The general motivation for coming was to improve oneself, just as with immigrants to English North America at various points in its history. Since the central areas turned out to have important accumulations of precious metals and the potential of producing much more, they had the capacity to pull immigrants in over the decades and centuries.

The process began with the conquering groups we have talked about. It was they who received the *encomiendas* and dominated the cities, building their large houses there and filling up the town councils. They could not do all that needed to be done by themselves, so immediately they started recruiting relatives and people from their home towns, promising help and employment. They brought many of the women of their own families to be married to their companions, to cement alliances and produce offspring who could perpetuate their position. The process soon snowballed, so that a whole, now local, Spanish population was appealing to relatives and compatriots in the homeland to come, building up a dense, complex Spanish social web which soon felt the need of fully organized governmental, ecclesiastical, and economic institutions.

Even so, there were not enough Spaniards for the tasks required. The wealth of the central areas made possible the importation of African slaves, who in some places almost came to rival the Spanish population in numbers. As domestic servants, artisans, labor bosses, and petty traders, they served as intermediaries between Spaniards and Indians. Nor were the Africans sufficient. Indigenous auxiliaries were used too, in ever increasing numbers. Through the *encomienda,* large numbers of them were frequently in the cities delivering tribute and doing short-term labor; some were commandeered to work for the Spaniards on a permanent basis. Many if not most male Spaniards had an Indian mistress-servant until such time as they should marry a Spanish woman (and perhaps beyond that point as well). The upshot was that the "Spanish" cities contained a growing population of blacks, Indians, and soon people of mixed blood, who shared varying degrees of Spanish culture.

Let us pick a few Spanish Peruvian names out of the anonymity of social processes to illustrate the rich variety of early Hispanic society in the central areas. María de Escobar was among the first Spanish women to reach Peru in the wake of the Conquest. She was not of high birth, for she lacked the title *doña* that noblewomen sported, but she had more education than most. She was one of the relatively few women of the time who even tried to sign her name. Moreover, she understood business—not only the general management of affairs, but complex financial dealings. She was married to three *encomenderos* of Lima, one after the other, each of higher social standing than

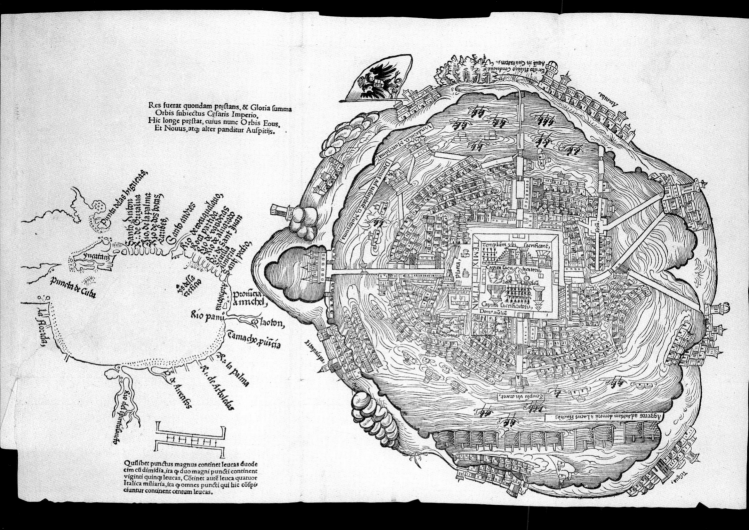

Res fuerat quondam preſtans, & Gloria ſumma
Orbis ſubiectus Ceſaris Imperio,
Hic longe preſtat, cuius nunc Orbis Eous,
Et Nouus, atq; alter panditur Auſpitijs.

Quiſlibet punctus magnus continet leucas duode
cim cū dimidia, ita q̄ duo magni puncti continent
viginti quinq; leucas, Cōtinet autē leuca quatuor
Italica miliaria, ita q̄ omnes puncti qui hic cōſpi
ciuntur continent centum leucas.

**Map of Mexico City and the Gulf of
Mexico. In Hernando Cortés. *Praeclara
Ferdinandi Cortesii de Nova maris Hys-
pania narratio*. [Norimbergae] [1524].
Rosenwald Collection, Rare Book and
Special Collections Division.**

This map, actually two separate maps on
one sheet, one of Tenochtitlán (Mexico
City) prepared by the Mexicas and presented to Cortés as a gift in the 1519–1521
period, and a map of the Gulf Coast region
of Mexico and the southeastern part of the
present-day United States, was prepared
either by the Mexica peoples or by a contemporary Spanish explorer.

Scene showing people of various ethnic backgrounds and indigenous animals of Peru. In Antonio de Ulloa. *Relación histórica del viage a la América meridional.* **Madrid, 1748. Rare Book and Special Collections Division.**

The assimilation of peoples of various races and cultures was one of the byproducts of the late fifteenth-century encounter of America and Europe. New foods, new animals, and new vegetation, to both Americans and Europeans, were exchanged. The potato, corn, tomato, cacao, pineapple, and alpacas from America made their way to Europe; Europe introduced the horse, cattle, pigs, and sugarcane.

the last, and she kept the same business connections and procedures through the whole time, becoming one of the wealthiest and best known people in the country. The *encomienda* and the establishment that went with it were actually more hers than her husbands'. Spanish women contributed mightily to social and cultural stability in their group in externally unsettled times.

At a lower level was Domingo de Destre, an Aragonese tailor who reached Lima on the eve of the great Indian rebellion of 1536–38 and spent the rest of his long life there. He worked in his trade from the beginning, but for a while he lived in the house of an *encomendero,* forming a relationship there with a black slave woman named Ana, by whom he had a child. Later he had an Indian mistress. He gradually built up one of the city's larger tailor shops (numerous blacks and Indians worked there) and also was an entrepreneur on the side. He repeatedly made plans to go back to Spain, but each new year found him still in Lima, where he stayed at least into his eighties. We do not know for sure if he ever married, but probably he did; at any rate, a Destre tailor shop was a feature of downtown Lima into the twentieth century.

At a yet lower rung was Juan de Fregenal, a black living in Lima in the 1540s and 50s. The freed slave of a notary, he had learned to sign his name, but to make a living he became a humble contractor, building adobe walls and other simple structures around the city. He was also a developer in a modest way, buying empty lots and gradually putting up houses on them, then selling them for much higher prices, and he went into truck gardening for the Lima market. He often dealt with Spaniards, sometimes as an equal, sometimes as an employee. He had a daughter by an Indian woman, but otherwise his social circle mainly consisted of other blacks and mulattoes. These three represent, of course, the merest hint of the flourishing Spanish and yet not quite Spanish society that was growing up in the midst of the Indian societies of the central areas.

What of those societies themselves? The very largest configurations, the "empires," were now gone, or rather replaced by the Spanish network. The local kingdoms had survived and, as we have seen, had been incorporated into the new framework through the *encomienda.* The *encomienda,* though the most basic, was far from the only institution the Spaniards built on indigenous structures. Once the potential of the regions was clear, the Spanish intention was to stay and rule permanently, introducing as much of their own way of doing things as was possible while keeping the indigenous base.

One thing they were serious about was their religious beliefs, which they wanted transferred in due course to Indian peoples. The concrete steps taken in that direction involved setting up churches and parishes in Indian areas; these, naturally enough, depended on the borders and internal mechanisms of the same kingdoms that supported the *encomienda,* and even to some extent on indigenous beliefs and practices, for the Indians fully expected to accept a conqueror's gods, and they were searching for close equivalents of their own ethnic deities. Christianity was thus usually quickly accepted on the surface, but often so reinterpreted that it was something very different.

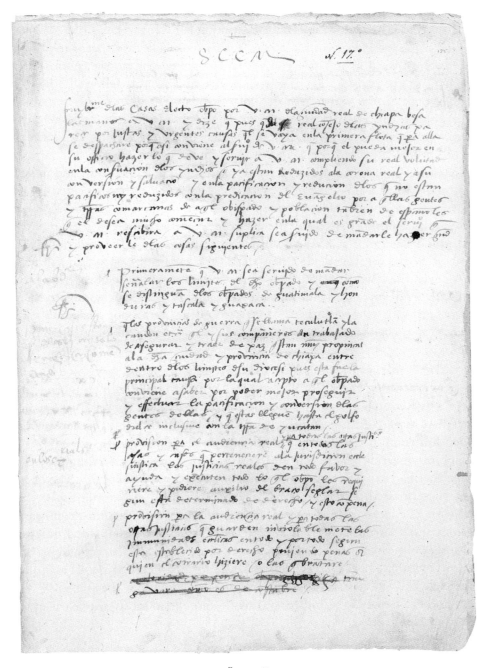

First page of the letter written by Fray Bartolomé de Las Casas to King Charles I shortly before he left Spain for America. 1542. Hans P. Kraus Collection. Manuscript Division.

We are indebted to the friar who abstracted Columbus's journal in his cramped and hurried style. The friar, who became a bishop, is known throughout history for his stand as champion of the rights of native Americans. Bartolomé de Las Casas spent sixty years tormenting his adversaries with the power of the Church; they in turn accused him of creating dissension and strife in the colonies. They accused him of ruining trade, discouraging emigration, and inciting the Indian peoples to rebellion.

Before leaving Spain to take the bishopric in Chiapas, New Spain, Las Casas penned, in 1542, in this same hurried style, a petition ostensibly to help enforce new laws promulgated in Spain, but actually to carry out his goal of improving the condition of Indian peoples. Las Casas had previously spent five years as a missionary, vicar, and a diocesan vicar in Central America, and now, as a high ecclesiastical official, could bring his years of experience to achieve his goal. As he prepared for his return trip to America, he presented thirty points for the governing Spanish *Consejo de las Indias,* concerning how bishops and friars could reform the issues of slavery, death, and rampant disregard for native life. The *Consejo* responded to each point, which was annotated in the margin.

Throughout his life, Las Casas wrote prolifically in Latin and in Spanish. His *Brevísima relación de la destrucción de las Indias* (1522) denigrated the Spanish colonial policies in America. After his six years as a bishop, impeaching judges and excommunicating refractory colonists, he resigned his post and returned to Spain where he continued to work within the Court towards his sole obsession: justice. As a participant-observer, he wrote the history of the Spanish colonization of America in his work *Historia general de las Indias,* enjoining it not to be published until long after his death for he realized that his criticisms were being used as propaganda by enemies of Spain; it appeared in print initially in 1875.

Not only was Las Casas the first priest ordained in America (1510), he was the first major American reformer. As a historian, he preserved the observations of Columbus. As a reformer, he refused to ignore the conquistadores' and subsequent colonists' injustices to Indian peoples of America.

Everette E. Larson

In sixteenth-century Europe, the key authoritative source of knowledge of the geography of America was based upon the work of the explorers and navigators, as interpreted and plotted by the official cosmographers and cartographers of the crowns of Spain and Portugal. Every pilot who accompanied an exploring expedition was under an obligation not only to keep a log but to make charts of sightings which had to be given to the authorities upon returning home. The *Casa de Contratación* (the Board of Trade) in Seville was the central authority for Spanish travel to America and custodian of charts and sailing directions of the Western Hemisphere. Diego Gutiérrez (born 1485 in Seville) was a chart maer, an instrument maker, and a pilot who worked in the *Casa de Contratación* from about 1534 until his death in 1554. His 1562 map of America was engraved by Hieronymus Cock, a talented Flemish artist born in Antwerp in 1510.

The Gutiérrez map, which relies upon the collection of data acquired by Spain on America, contains the most up-to-date information on the people, settlements, and other geographical features of the Atlantic and Gulf coasts of North America, all of Central and South America, and portions of the western coasts of Africa. Although no coordinates appear, the map details an area roughly between 0 and 115 degrees longitude west of Greenwich and 57 degrees north and 70 degrees south latitude. Six separately engraved sheets are neatly joined to form the largest printed map of the Western Hemisphere up to that time (36 ¾ inches by 33 ½ inches).

The map provides a grand view of an America filled with images and names that had been popularized in Europe over seventy years: parrots, monkeys, mermaids, huge sea creatures, Brazilian cannibals, Patagonian giants, and an erupting volcano in central Mexico complement settlements, rivers, mountains, and capes. Although containing fanciful imagery, Gutiérrez's map did correctly recognize the existence of the Amazon River system, other rivers of South America, Lake Titicaca, the location of Potosí, and the myriad coastal features of South, Central, North, and Caribbean America. It was the last printed Spanish map of America to appear before the late seventeenth century.

Another dimension of Spanish interest was local government, which after an interval of relying entirely on indigenous forms they tried to reshape according to their own norms. Essentially, they tried to turn the local kingdoms into Spanish-style municipalities with town councils. The reform indeed took hold, but it was necessary to give an important role in the new arrangement to the traditional ruler, and all the offices tended to be held by the same indigenous noblemen who were the officeholders before the conquest; moreover, they represented jurisdictions and operated through rotation and subdivision much as in preconquest times. In both religion and government in the indigenous world, some truly new elements were introduced; but much of what appeared to be "introduced" was virtually identical to what was already there and was accepted for that very reason; and a great deal that was quite different from the Spanish version persisted, often quite unnoticed.

The dialectics of change and persistence went on not only in religious and political matters, but everywhere in the indigenous sector. Language, culture, social organization, and the economy all went through the same experience. To take an example again, let us look at a case that came to the attention of the Indian town council of Tulancingo, in northeastern central Mexico, in the early 1580s. The two principals, humble fellows both, were named only Simón and Cristóbal, both Spanish-Christian names. Cristóbal had stolen a turkey from Simón's house by night, leading to an altercation. In the process we learn that they had house complexes very much like those of the preconquest era, grew indigenous crops, spoke in a rhetoric familiar from earlier times, had the same relationship to local authorities, and in general maintained a life-style one might imagine was nearly unaffected by the presence of Spaniards. But on close inspection, we find in Simón's Nahuatl complaint a number of words taken from Spanish, which in turn point to cultural influence. The Spanish seven-day week is in use; the traditional digging stick has an iron blade; men wear their traditional cloak and some of them even the older loincloth, but to that has been added the European fitted and buttoned shirt. In the houses are Spanish-style wooden chests with metal latches, as well as steel knives. Money is known, being borrowed and paid. Before long, then, cultural contact was affecting every level and dimension of the indigenous world, with many different results.

One result, in the long run, was that the Spanish and indigenous orbits, though remaining recognizably separate, began to grow into each other and form a new overall entity, the proto-form of the nations we see in the region today. As disease diminished the Indian sector until the time, centuries later, when full immunities were acquired, and the Hispanic sector grew through biological increase and racial and cultural mixture, much changed in the scene that had existed in the generation or two after the Conquest. The *encomienda* deteriorated, giving way to other estate forms; silver mining became the basis of a large-scale, highly technical industry with vast financial implications and a far-flung support system; land values increased; social differentiation became more complex and ambiguous; regional dialects and artistic styles grew up; a new kind of consciousness formed. Through it all and until our days, the old central areas have retained the stamp of the sixteenth century and the flavor of the indigenous world more than most other parts of the Western Hemisphere.

The map, one of only two known copies
to exist, was given to the Library of Congress by Lessing J. Rosenwald.

John R. Hébert

Négresses allant à l'Eglise, pour être baptisées. Engraving. By Jean-Baptiste Debret. *Voyage pittoresque et historique au Brésil,* **Vol. 3. Paris, 1839. Rare Book and Special Collections Division.**

Africans, who were brought to Brazil as slaves to work on plantations in increasing numbers from the late 1500s, comprised an important part of the population and contributed significantly to the wealth and uniqueness of Brazilian culture. In his encyclopedic multivolume *Voyage Pittoresque . . . au Brésil,* Debret stresses the pivotal role played by blacks as the backbone upon which Brazilian society and economy rested. Thus Debret devotes many plates and text to them, such as this one depicting black women on their way to church to be baptized. In this illustration, young slave women with infants are shepherded by older slaves, the godmother and the godfather, to a church. The viewer is struck at once by the contrast of the elaborate dress and costume with the bare feet of some of the protagonists. It is noteworthy that the portly priest holding a tobacco pouch is also black, because as Debret observed, there were in Rio de Janeiro, by the early 1800s, at least three churches served by free black priests.[1] Thus this work expresses a fusion of cultures and beliefs that came to typify Brazil in the years after the Portuguese Conquest.

Forced to flee the Napoleonic Wars in Europe, the Portuguese regent, Dom João, chose to transfer his monarchy and court to the Portuguese colony of Brazil. In early 1808, they arrived in Rio de Janeiro. Interested in remodelling Rio de Janeiro along French neoclassical lines, Dom João invited a prominent group of French planners, architects, and artists, under the leadership of Le Breton, to Rio de Janeiro in 1816.

Among the talented group was the artist Jean-Baptiste Debret (1768–1848), a cousin

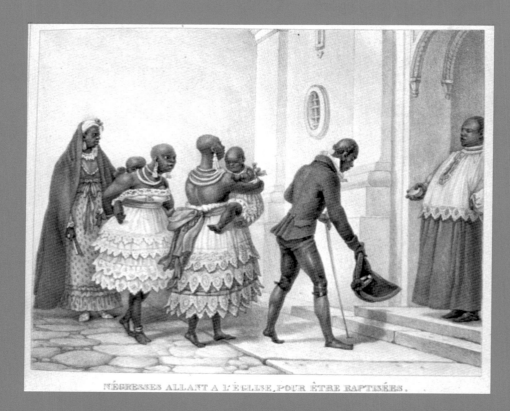

NÉGRESSES ALLANT A L'ÉGLISE, POUR ÊTRE BAPTISÉES.

of two celebrated French artists, François Boucher and Jacques Louis David, the latter serving as court painter to Napoleon. Under the influence of David, Debret frequented the Académie des Beaux Arts. Because of his association with David and Napoleon, Debret's career and future were uncertain when Napoleon fell in 1815. This prompted him to accept an assignment with the Le Breton Mission.

Quality and meticulous observation characterize the numerous drawings, sketches, and watercolors, that Debret made during the eight years that he worked and travelled in Brazil as court painter to the Braganza family and as "cataloger of the imperial family's human subjects and its physical do-

main in the New World."[2] Debret also relied on written documents to assist him in recording minutely and accurately the myriad customs, occupations, dress, and festivals of the diverse population (indigenous, blacks, and whites).

Anthony Páez Mullan

Notes

1. Jean-Baptiste Debret. *Viagem Pitoresca e Historica ao Brasil* (tomo II, vol. III). Tradução e notas de Sergio Milliet (São Paulo: Editora da Universidade de São Paulo, 1978), pp. 166–69.

2. Dawn Ades et al. *Art in Latin America: The Modern Era, 1820–1980* (New Haven: Yale University, 1989), p. 48.

CHAPTER NINE

EPILOGUE

by BARBARA M. LOSTE

"In any negotiation,
the important thing at the
outset is to declare and
recognize one's own
value system, which is the
ultimate meaning
of tolerance."

RICARDO DÍEZ HOCHLEITNER

HE 1990 U.S. CENSUS reveals that, while Asian and Hispanic segments of the population are the fastest growing national minorities, ten million U.S. citizens consider themselves "other race," or not definable within the categories established by the Census Bureau. How we define ourselves seems an increasingly unruly task: whether by race, ethnicity, cultural preference, or individual heritage. And yet this phenomenon is not without precedent. The Western Hemisphere was the scene of numerous conquests throughout the sixteenth century, prompting the continuous immigration of Europeans of diverse cultural origins. The indigenous populations responded to and associated with these arrivals in different ways, and the arena for interaction between peoples of distinct cultural and racial backgrounds was created. During this period, African peoples from diverse ethnic, religious, and social groups also crossed the Atlantic, often enslaved or as indentured workers, to become partners—albeit unwillingly—in the shaping of the New World. This complex process set the stage for the multiracial, multicultural societies that exist in the hemisphere today.

Immigration to the territorial United States, where hundreds of distinct Indian Nations traditionally exercised control over the territory, dates from 1513 with the arrival of Juan Ponce de León to Florida. During his search through the Florida Keys, where he purportedly was looking for the Fountain of Youth, he inadvertently encountered an abundance of herons, flamingoes, alligators, and turtles. In the process, he also came up against the Calusa Nation. The Spanish later established a permanent settlement in 1565 at St. Augustine, Florida, territory of the Timucua Indians. By 1570, a Spanish mission was in place in Ajacan territory near present-day Williamsburg, Virginia, predating Jamestown and John Smith by thirty-seven years. Foreign immigration to the United States continues today with the steady arrival of peoples from diverse continents and cultures, often seeking the same things as those who preceded them: a better life and greater cultural freedom.

The German mapmaker Martin Waldseemüller has been credited with the naming of America. In his 1507 printed world map, Waldseemüller honored the Italian navigator and explorer Amerigo Vespucci by placing the word "America" on a landmass which turned out not to be Asia, as had been expected, but a vast continent separating Europe from the Orient. Historically speaking, therefore, all of the inhabitants of the Western Hemisphere are Americans, even though in English-speaking America today the word is mostly used to signify people of the territorial United States. However, many people of this hemisphere also think of themselves generically as Americans. They have been taught from childhood that there is but one American continent, generally subdivided between substantially Anglo-Saxon dominant areas (the United States and parts of Canada) and what is now commonly referred to as Latin America, largely but not totally Spanish-speaking. As the prominent Colombian historian Germán Arciniegas suggests, the ambiguity of the word "American" has no parallel in any other region of the world.

The Naming of America. In Martin Waldseemüller. *Cosmographiae introductio.* **St. Dié, 1507. Thacher Collection, Rare Book and Special Collections Division.**

As is well known, America was the name given to the Western Hemisphere in the early sixteenth century in honor of Amerigo Vespucci's recognition that a "New World," the so-called fourth part of the world, had been reached through Columbus's voyage. Before that time, there was no name that collectively identified the Western Hemisphere. The earlier Spanish explorers referred to the area as the Indies believing, as did Columbus, that it was part of eastern Asia.

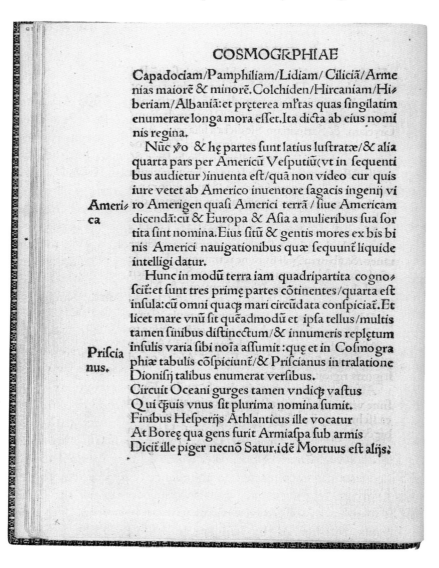

Retablo de Nuestro Señor de Esquipula, Chimayo, New Mexico [Altar Screen]. Watercolor. In *Historic American Buildings Survey*. 1934. Prints and Photographs Division.

Little is known of the history of the church of the Santuario. It was commissioned by Bernardo Abeyta and was completed by 1816.[1] Since that time the site has become associated with miraculous cures. Although this adobe church was built relatively recently, its construction and decoration adhere to a pattern of missionary church building found elsewhere in New Mexico that ultimately has its roots in the early church architecture of Mexico. From the 1520s to about 1570, the mendicant orders were in charge of church building. A particular characteristic of many of these structures was their aisleless nave, probably for reasons of military protection. Another feature of both early churches in Mexico and later ones in New Mexico is that they were built of varying amounts of stone and adobe.[2]

Altar screens, like the one depicted in this illustration, are especially ornate in their design and fabrication. Their complexity is perhaps best revealed in Spanish America (specifically Mexico) where there was some fusion of indigenous expression with European elements.

This elaborate and intricately designed altar screen may have been painted by Molleno, sometimes known as the "Chili Painter," whose career spanned the period 1804 to 1845.[3] The screen is conceived of as a stagelike space that focuses on the tabernacle frame. Colorful abstract bands and loops and simulated curtains frame illustrations of various Christian symbols and icons. According to Marina Ochoa (Archdiocese of Santa Fe), we have, in the upper register from left to right, symbolic representations of (1) the Holy Cross with the five wounds of Jesus and the lance, (2) the Franciscan emblem with the arm of St. Francis crossing that of Christ, and (3) the so-called Cross of Jerusalem or Cross of the Holy Sepulchre. In the lower register on the left, wheat is depicted representing symbolically the bread of the Last Supper, while on the right a bunch of grapes signifies the wine.

The church is associated with the cult of the Señor of Esquipula that emphasized Christ's healing and miraculous powers. The cult was initiated in Guatemala toward the end of the sixteenth century after a pe-

While in many ways seemingly new, America was actually quite old, even in 1492. Sophisticated agricultural methods, astronomy, commerce, sea travel, city building, organized religion, and architectural design had been known for centuries by pre-Conquest American civilizations. These civilizations had also known internal conflicts, war, and disease. With the arrival of Europe to America, significant changes were to take place. The introduction of animals and plants such as the horse, wheat, and sugar cane dramatically altered the face of indigenous societies and the use of the land. European vernaculars such as Spanish, French, Portuguese, English, and Dutch would eventually supplant or mix with hundreds of Indian languages. Indeed, the entire world was significantly transformed when "exotic" New World products such as cacao, tomatoes, potatoes, chiles, corn, and tobacco were introduced abroad. Today, it would be difficult to imagine a world without access to these indigenous American food products: there would be no cornbread, no vodka, no fried potatoes, no chocolate, and, alas, no ketchup.

One hundred years ago, President Grover Cleveland auspiciously inaugurated the extravagant 1893 World's Columbian Exposition in Chicago,

riod of strife and turbulence between civil and ecclesiastical authorities.

Anthony Páez Mullan

Notes

1. George Kubler. *The Religious Architecture of New Mexico in the Colonial Period and since the American Occupation* (Albuquerque: University of New Mexico Press, 1972) (4th printing), p. 104.

2. For a brief, perceptive outline of the mendicant orders and missionary architecture in early colonial Mexico and New Mexico see Kubler, 1972, pp. 4–32.

3. Robert J. Stroessner, "Folk Art of Spanish New Mexico," in *How to Know American Folk Art: Eleven Experts Discuss Many Aspects of the Field* (New York: E. P. Dutton, 1977), p. 74.

Carnaval Ponce de León. Half tone and lithographed poster. By Oscar Colón Delgado [Puerto Rico]. 1939. Prints and Photographs Division.

Carnival originated in Europe in the Middle Ages to portend the start of Christian Lent and symbolically celebrate the death of winter and the beginning of spring.

The earliest modern recording of Carnival in Puerto Rico was 1902. These Carnivals, referred to as *carnaval callejero* lacked formal structure. People donned a wide variety of costumes and masks and surged through the streets marching, singing, and dancing. They pretended to attack houses and waged feigned warfare in the streets with water balloons, fruit peels, and pots of water. Carnival ended at sunset on Shrove Tuesday or Mardi Gras.[1]

This early Carnival underwent many changes, until 1937, when the governor of Puerto Rico, Blanton Winship, recommended the return to a more spectacular presentation—based on the grander European Carnival tradition, which included pageantry. He reasoned that these celebrations could be used to promote tourism and encourage economic development. The governor proposed that these new "spectacular" Carnivals be named after Juan Ponce de León (1460?-1521), the first governor of Puerto Rico. Winship recommended that in order to give Carnival a national character, a young *embajadora* should be selected from each of the island's seven districts. From among these seven ambassadresses, a panel of judges would select Queen Borinquen, after the original name of Puerto Rico. The queen then chose the king of the Carnival.[2]

which celebrated with much fanfare the 400th anniversary of Columbus's "Discovery of America." A century later, a lengthy list of activities and programs have been planned throughout the world for the Columbus Quincentenary, often reflecting a tone closer to examination and reflection than celebration. These include a variety of educational programs, publications, regattas, television series, films, exhibits, scholarships, and academic conferences. They not only touch upon Columbus-related themes, such as further inquiry into the specifics of his life and nautical achievements, but also broader academic research on subjects including the nature of America at the time of contact, indigenous responses to conquest, European and African immigration to the Western Hemisphere, and scientific exchanges between Europe-Africa-Asia and America. In many countries, the programs designed for the 1992 Quincentenary have been met with heightened interest but also, in some cases, with some controversy. During 1992, many ships will come and go. And, yet, what will remain?

CARNAVAL PONCE DE LEON
PUERTO RICO
del 9 al 21 de Febrero de 1939
GRAN ILUMINACION – PARADAS
DESFILES – VERBENAS – FUEGOS ARTIFICIALES
13 dias de grandes fiestas
VISITE A SAN JUAN.

This profuse medley of interests and focuses puts an unavoidable spotlight upon one of the most pressing legacies of the original Caribbean event half a millennium ago: the history of today's multicultural populations. For some, renewed emphasis on multiculturalism connotes upheaval and the erosion of civilization. For others, it is seen as a possibility for greater self awareness and, conceivably, a heightened sense of identity. Still others, who have struggled to keep their cultures intact and perceive their history as continuous, view increased tolerance towards multiculturalism as a long-awaited opportunity to pursue their cultural values more freely. Indeed, in the Western Hemisphere—where *mestizo* or *métis* populations have flourished and different forms of cultural coexistence have become commonplace—each of these viewpoints has found room for expression.

The Columbus Quincentenary is ultimately about America—from South to North—and the complex process that was initiated on October 12, 1492, when a group of Mediterranean navigators touched soil in the Caribbean and claimed both land and inhabitants for the glory of their royal patrons. The story that has been taught traditionally in school has suggested that the dramatic history of the hemisphere began with this European "discovery of America." From the point of view of men and women whose religious and cultural institutions derive directly from Europe, this way of understanding history has seemed natural, even inevitable. Our "Ongoing Voyage" does not ignore this perspective but tries to move beyond it by examining, in something of its rich and sometimes baffling complexity, the background and nature of the meeting of Europeans and Americans that took place 500 years ago. With the landings of Christopher Columbus in America, the likelihood of a multicultural, multiracial, multiethnic hemisphere was virtually guaranteed. The seeds planted then have grown and multiplied over the past 500 years. It is to be hoped that the commemorative events of 1992 will lead to a deeper appreciation of our global heritage, so that we may live with more understanding within the cultural diversity that is our legacy today.

The poster shown here was made for the third Carnaval Ponce de León, which was truly a spectacular event. Juan Ponce de León had been sent to Puerto Rico in 1508 by Nicolás de Ovando, Spanish governor of Santo Domingo, to explore, conquer, and colonize the island. He established relations with Aqueybana, chief of the Arawak Indians who lived on the island, and with his acquiescence founded a Spanish settlement, Villa de Caparra, which was later renamed Ciudad de Porto Rico. This poster is the earliest in a collection of approximately three hundred Puerto Rican posters, dating from 1937 to 1989, in the Library's collection. It was created by Oscar Colón Delgado (1889–1968), a self-taught artist, born in Hatillo, Puerto Rico, who earned international recognition through his paintings and sculptures. Oscar Colón's realist landscapes, portraits, and genre scenes were inspired by his beloved country. In 1967, the year before his death, he was honored by a retrospective exhibition for having done much to "keep alive Puerto Rico's artistic tradition."[3]

Elena G. Millie

Notes

1. Adolfo De Hostos. *Diccionario Histórico Bibliográfico Comentado de Puerto Rico* (San Juan: Academia Puertorriqueña de la Historia, 1976), p. 232.

2. Ibid., p. 233.

3. Peter Bloch. *Painting and Sculpture of the Puerto Ricans* (New York: Plus Ultra Educational Publishers, Inc., 1978), p. 170.

Tejedoras y mercaderas de sombreros nacuma en Bucamaranga. Tipo blanco, mestizo, y zambo. [Illustration of original watercolor by Carmelo Fernández] 1850. In *Acuarelas de la Comisión Corográfica: Colombia 1850–59*. Bogotá, 1986. General Collections.

Fernández's exciting watercolor paintings of Colombian life, with their mixed racial hues, are testimony to the process of change that had taken place in America following the encounter of America with Europe in 1492.

Facing page: **Carnival Dominica [San Pedro de Macoris]. Drawing in watercolor and gouache over charcoal on brown wove paper [poster]. By George Overbury "Pop" Hart [Santo Domingo, 1919]. Prints and Photographs Division.**

Like other Caribbean festivals, Carnival in the Dominican Republic in 1919 was the site of the mingling of African and Old World cultures. A celebration which for centuries has marked the last fling before the Lenten season in much of the Christian world, Carnival took on a totally different, syncretic character in the Caribbean. British folk mummery, the European tradition of masquerade, and the commedia dell'arte here blended with many features from African performance and spectacle arts. "Carnival Dominica" shows the arrival of a riotous Carnival band, with its costumed kettle drum, horn, and accordion players, in a small village. The stilt dancer Moco Jumbie, prominent in this band, was a character introduced throughout the Caribbean by slaves and free immigrants from Sierra Leone and other West African nations. Cowhead, here seen at far left, was by the time of this drawing a fixture of the African-inspired Jonkonnu festivals.

Hart's work is a record of Carnival as it was enacted in the Dominican Republic in 1919, an inheritance of the colonial encounter between European and African cultures. The drawing itself, however, is also a document of another encounter: between a North American artist and the Caribbean world. George Overbury Hart was a painter, born and trained in the United States. Life in rural Dominican Republic as seen through his eyes was conditioned by a number of cultural and political forces operative in turn-of-the-century United States, forces which set the terms for this particular encounter.

Hart ventured into the Caribbean at a time when modern art was engaged in a search for the primitive, for culture unspoiled by the detritus of modern industrial civilization. Avant-garde Western artists, like Pablo Picasso and Georges Braque, were beginning to explore the formal qualities of non-Western arts as a means of escaping the strictures of academic conventions and traditions. The forms of African sculpture would inspire Picasso just as the Japanese print had inspired Degas and Whistler before him. This interest in less developed parts of the world was also driven by a romantic quest for exotic subjects and faraway places. This quest had led

Hart as early as 1903 to Haiti, Trinidad, and Mexico, and to the South Sea Islands in the footsteps of painter Paul Gauguin and U.S. writer Robert Louis Stevenson.

In his portrayals of Caribbean life, Hart's involvement went beyond what one would expect of a painter of his time. Hart worked his passage. He lived with his subjects, participated in their daily rituals, and learned first hand their customs. Given this, it is not surprising that his "Carnival Dominica" and other works capture a sense, if not of the people themselves, of the rhythms of Caribbean life.

Bernard Reilly

Further Reading

Douglas Dreishpoon and Susan E. Menconi. *The Arts of the American Renaissance* (New York: Hirschl and Adler, 1985).

Gregory Gilbert. *George Overbury "Pop" Hart: His Life and Art* (New Brunswick: Rutgers University Press, 1986).

John W. Nunley and Judith Bettelheim. *Caribbean Festival Arts* (Seattle: University of Washington Press, 1988).

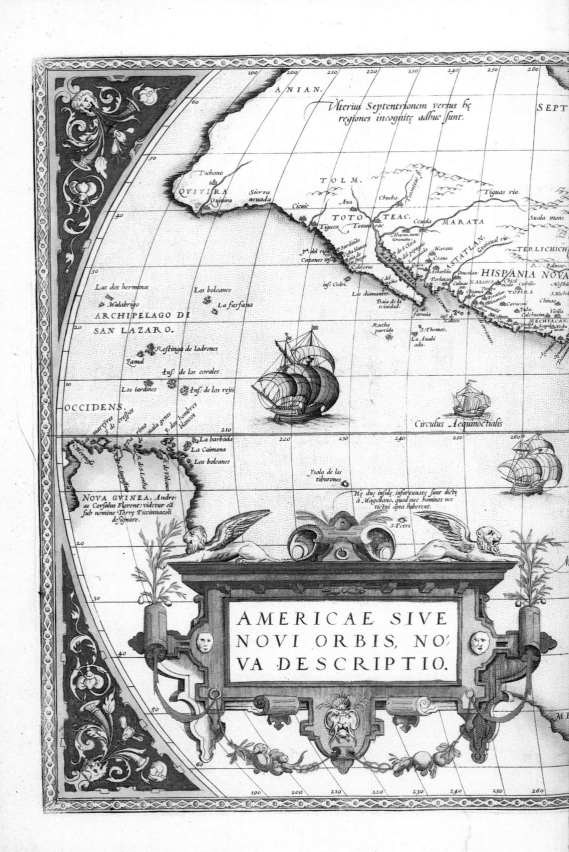

Americae Sive Novi Orbis, Nova Descriptio [America Map]. In Ortelius. *Theatrum Orbis Terrarum.* Antwerp, 1570. Geography and Map Division.

European scholarship slowly realized that an entirely distinctive part of the world had been reached by Columbus in 1492. This map by Ortelius is one of the first to acknowledge a Western Hemisphere, especially the North American segment, separate from Asia.

JUGGEJTIONJ FOR FURTHER READING

CHAPTER 2: INTELLECTUAL LIFE IN THE MEDITERRANEAN WORLD

Braudel, Fernand. *The Mediterranean and the Mediterranean World in the Age of Phillip II,* 2 vols. (New York: Harper and Row, 1972).

Huizinga, Johannes. *The Waning of the Middle Ages* (Garden City, N.Y.: Doubleday Anchor Books, 1954).

Prescott, William H. *History of the Reign of Ferdinand and Isabella the Catholic* (Philadelphia: Lippincott, 1864).

CHAPTER 3: SPAIN IN THE ERA OF EXPLORATION

Altman, Ida. *Emigrants and Society: Extremadura and America in the Sixteenth Century* (Berkeley: University of California Press, 1989).

Christian, William A. *Local Religion in Sixteenth-century Spain* (Princeton: Princeton University Press, 1981).

Elliott, John Huxtable. *Imperial Spain, 1469–1716* (Hammondsworth: Penguin, 1970).

Kagan, Richard L. *Students and Society in Early Modern Spain* (Baltimore: Johns Hopkins University Press, 1974).

Kamen, Henry A. F. *Inquisition and Society in Spain in the Sixteenth and Seventeenth Centuries* (Bloomington: Indiana University Press, 1985).

MacKay, Angus. *Spain in the Middle Ages: From Frontier to Empire, 1000–1500* (New York: St. Martin's Press, 1977).

Pike, Ruth. *Aristocrats and Traders: Sevillian Society in the Sixteenth Century* (Ithaca: Cornell University Press, 1972).

Saunders, A. C. de C. M. *A Social History of Black Slaves and Freedom in Portugal, 1441–1555* (New York: Cambridge University Press, 1982).

Vassberg, David E. *Land and Society in Golden Age Castile* (New York: Cambridge University Press, 1984).

CHAPTER 4: MAPS, NAVIGATION, AND WORLD TRAVEL

Cortesão, Armando. *History of Portuguese Cartography* (Lisbon: Investigações da Junta Ultramar, 1969–71).

Harley, J. B. and Woodward, David, ed. *History of Cartography,* vol. 1 (Chicago: University of Chicago Press, 1987).

Hewson, J. B. *A History of the Practice of Navigation* (Glasgow: Brown, Son and Ferguson, 1951).

May, W. E. *A History of Maritime Navigation* (Henley on Thames, England: G. T. Foulis and Co., 1973).

Olschki, Leonardo. *Marco Polo's Asia* (Berkeley: University of California Press, 1960).

Rogers, Francis M. *The Travels of the Infante Dom Pedro of Portugal* (Cambridge, Mass.: Harvard University Press, 1961).

Taylor, E. G. R. *The Haven-finding Art* (London: Hollis and Carter for the Institute of Navigation, 1971).

Waters, David W. *The Art of Navigation in England in Elizabethan and Early Stuart Times* (New Haven: Yale University Press, 1958).

Zacher, Christian. *Curiosity and Pilgrimage: The Literature of Discovery in Fourteenth-century England* (Baltimore: Johns Hopkins University Press, 1976).

CHAPTER 5: CHRISTOPHER COLUMBUS, THE MAN AND THE MYTH

Colón, Fernando. *The Life of Admiral Christopher Columbus by His Son Ferdinand,* trans. Benjamin Keen (Westport, Conn.: Greenwood Press, 1959).

Dunn, Oliver and Kelley, James, ed. *The Diario of Christopher Columbus's First Voyage to America, 1492–1493* (Norman: University of Oklahoma Press, 1989).

Madariaga, Salvador de. *Christopher Columbus* (Westport, Conn.: Greenwood Press, 1979).

Milhou, Alain. *Colón y su mentalidad mesianica en el ambiente franciscanista español* (Valladolid: Casa-Museo de Colón; Seminario Americanista de la Universidad de Valladolid, 1983).

Morison, Samuel Eliot. *Admiral of the Ocean Sea: A Life of Christopher Columbus* (Boston: Little, Brown and Co., 1942).

Pérez de Tudela y Bueso, Juan. *Mirabilis in altis: estudio crítico sobre el origen y significado del proyecto descubridor de Crístobal Colón* (Madrid: Consejo Superior de Investigaciones Científicas, Instituto "Gonzalo Fernández de Oviedo," 1983).

Sale, Kirkpatrick. *The Conquest of Paradise: Christopher Columbus and the Columbian Legacy* (New York: Alfred A. Knopf, 1990).

Taviani, Paolo Emilio. *Christoforo Colombo: la genesi della grande scoperta* (Novara: Instituto geografico de Agostini, 1982).

Varela, Consuelo, ed. *Crístobal Colón; textos y documentos completos/relaciónes de viajes, cartas y memoriales* (Madrid: Alianza, 1982).

CHAPTER 6: THE INDIANS OF THE CENTRAL AREAS WHEN THE EUROPEANS ARRIVED

Berdan, Frances F. *The Aztecs of Central Mexico* (New York: Holt, Rinehart and Winston, 1982).

Cieza de Leon, Pedro. *The Incas* (Norman: University of Oklahoma Press, 1959).

Collier, George A., ed. *The Inca and Aztec States, 1400–1800* (New York: Academic Press, 1982).

Katz, Friedrich. *The Ancient American Civilizations* (New York: Praeger, 1972).

León-Portilla, Miguel. *Aztec Thought and Culture* (Norman: University of Oklahoma Press, 1963).

Murra, John V. *The Economic Organization of the Inca State* (Greenwich, Conn.: JAI Press, 1980).

Zuidema, R. Tom. *Inca Civilization in Cuzco* (Austin: University of Texas Press, 1990).

CHAPTER 7: THE CONTACT OF CULTURES IN AMERICA

Caribbean

Floyd, Troy S. *The Columbus Dynasty in the Caribbean: 1492–1526* (Albuquerque: University of New Mexico Press, 1973).

Knight, Franklin W. *The Caribbean, the Genesis of a Fragmented Nationalism* (New York: Oxford University Press, 1990).

Sauer, Carl O. *The Early Spanish Main* (Berkeley: University of California Press, 1969).

Wilson, Samuel M. *Hispaniola: Caribbean Chiefdoms in the Age of Columbus* (Tuscaloosa: University of Alabama, 1990).

North America

Axtell, James. *The Invasion Within: The Conquest of Cultures in Colonial North America* (New York: Oxford University Press, 1985).

Gutiérrez, Ramón A. *When Jesus Came, the Corn Mothers Went Away: Marriage, Sexuality, and Power in New Mexico, 1500–1846* (Stanford: Stanford University Press, 1991).

Nash, Gary B. *Red, White, and Black: The Peoples of Early America* (Englewood Cliffs, N.J.: Prentice-Hall, 1982).

Sauer, Carl O. *Sixteenth Century North America* (Berkeley: University of California Press, 1971).

Spicer, Edward H. *Cycles of Conquest: The Impact of Spain, Mexico, and the United States on the Indians of the Southwest, 1533–1690* (Tucson: University of Arizona Press, 1967).

Swanton, John R. *The Indians of the South-eastern United States* (Washington, D.C.: Smithsonian Institution Press, 1946).

Brazil and Atlantic South America

Hemming, John. *Red Gold: The Conquest of the Brazilian Indians, 1500–1760* (Cambridge, Mass.: Harvard University Press, 1978).

Lockhart, James and Schwartz, Stuart B. *Early Latin America* (Cambridge: Cambridge University Press, 1983).

Marchant, Alexander N. *From Barter to Slavery: The Economic Relations of Portuguese and Indians in the Settlement of Brazil 1500–1580* (Baltimore: Johns Hopkins University Press, 1942).

Service, Elman R. *Spanish-Guarani Relations in Early Colonial Paraguay* (Westport: Greenwood Press, 1971).

CHAPTER 8: THE CENTRAL AREAS DURING AND AFTER THE CONQUEST

Gardiner, C. Harvey. *Naval Power in the Conquest of Mexico* (Austin: University of Texas Press, 1956).

Hemming, John. *The Conquest of the Incas* (New York: Harcourt Brace Jovanovich, 1970).

Lockhart, James. *Spanish Peru, 1532–1560* (Madison: University of Wisconsin Press, 1968).

————— *The Men of Cajamarca* (Austin: University of Texas Press, 1972).

————— *The Nahuas After the Conquest* (Stanford: Stanford University Press, 1992).

————— and Otte, Enrique, eds. *Letters and People of the Spanish Indies* (Cambridge: Cambridge University Press, 1976).

Sahagún, Bernardino de, Fray, comp. *The War of Conquest: How It Was Waged Here in Mexico* (Arthur J. O. Anderson and Charles E. Dibble, tr. and ed. (Salt Lake City: University of Utah Press, 1978).

ABOUT THE AUTHORS

Ida Altman is Guest Curator, 1492: An Ongoing Voyage, and Professor of History, University of New Orleans.

George N. Atiyeh is Head, Near East Section, African and Middle Eastern Division, Library of Congress.

Reid S. Baker is Senior Photographer, Photoduplication Service, Library of Congress.

Ralph E. Ehrenberg is Chief, Geography and Map Division, Library of Congress.

Kathryn L. Engstrom is Senior Reference Librarian, Geography and Map Division, Library of Congress.

James A. Flatness is Head, Acquisitions Unit, Geography and Map Division, Library of Congress.

John Fleming is Guest Curator, 1492: An Ongoing Voyage, and Fairchild Professor of English, Princeton University.

James Gilreath is American History Specialist, Rare Book and Special Collections Division, Library of Congress.

John R. Hébert is Curator, 1492: An Ongoing Voyage, Coordinator, The Quincentenary Program, and Assistant Chief, Hispanic Division, Library of Congress.

James Higgins is Senior Photographer, Photoduplication Service, Library of Congress.

Everette E. Larson is Head, Reference Section, Hispanic Division, Library of Congress.

James Lockhart is Professor of History, University of California, Los Angeles.

Barbara M. Loste is Exhibit Director, 1492: An Ongoing Voyage, and Associate Coordinator, The Quincentenary Program, Library of Congress.

Lee K. Miller is Indian Peoples' Research Specialist, The Quincentenary Program, Library of Congress.

Elena G. Millie is Curator, Poster Collection, Prints and Photographs Division, Library of Congress.

Anthony Páez Mullan is Librarian and Fine Arts Reference Specialist, General Reading Rooms Division and Visual Research Specialist, The Quincentenary Program, Library of Congress.

Rosemary Fry Plakas is American History Specialist, Rare Book and Special Collections Division, Library of Congress.

Bernard Reilly is Head, Curatorial Collection, Prints and Photographs Division, Library of Congress.

Robert L. Roy is Researcher and Office Manager, The Quincentenary Program, Library of Congress.

Richard W. Stephenson was Specialist in American Cartographic History, Geography and Map Division, Library of Congress, until he retired in January 1992.

Peter Van Wingen is Specialist for Book Arts, Rare Book and Special Collections Division, Library of Congress.

John A. Wolter was Chief, Geography and Map Division, Library of Congress, until he retired in August 1991.

INDEX

Illustrations appear on **boldfaced** pages.

ISBN 0-16-036182-6